Chaos

Morgan Harris

Chaos

Olympia Publishers
London

www.olympiapublishers.com
OLYMPIA PAPERBACK EDITION

Copyright © Morgan Harris 2024

The right of Morgan Harris to be identified as author of this work has been asserted in accordance with sections 77 and 78 of the Copyright, Designs and Patents Act 1988.

All Rights Reserved

No reproduction, copy or transmission of this publication may be made without written permission. No paragraph of this publication may be reproduced, copied or transmitted save with the written permission of the publisher, or in accordance with the provisions of the Copyright Act 1956 (as amended).

Any person who commits any unauthorised act in relation to this publication may be liable to criminal prosecution and civil claims for damage.

A CIP catalogue record for this title is available from the British Library.

ISBN: 978-1-80439-977-4

This book is memoir. It reflects the author's present recollections of experiences over time. Some names and characteristics have been changed, some events have been compressed, and some dialogue has been recreated.

First Published in 2024

Olympia Publishers
Tallis House
2 Tallis Street
London
EC4Y 0AB

Printed in Great Britain

Hi, I'm Morgan, and I'm the guy every guy seems to date but never really dated.

Obviously, dating is hard... for everyone. Being a gay man is hard. Being a gay man who doesn't drink much is hard. Being the gay guy who happily dates people, but they never end up being the love of someone else's life is hard. Why wasn't it ever me?

I've dated many guys. Some great, some shocking, some absolutely terrifyingly abysmal. But the ones that get the second, third, fourth, fifth dates, they're good... to me. I don't like to put myself fully out there, like most people, but I also don't like to resist the opportunity to meet someone if the... spark... thing... whatever it is, is there. I go with it. I really try to put myself out there where I can, to show that I'm willing to give it a go and be open. I've had short-term flings, long-term things, and some for years, whatever you'd call that, but never to the point of calling someone my 'boyfriend' and when brought up, it kills the 'whatever this thing is' vibe entirely as I start to see 'whatever it was' start to rot like the houseplant you just for some reason CANNOT keep alive.

I chronically fall into situationships. You know, where it's more than a thing, but not branded a relationship. Where you're literally acting like boyfriends already before actually calling each other boyfriends. And when it ends, because technically you never were boyfriends, you always kind of wonder, what if? You're left on a cliff-hanger wondering if it'll ever end up happening in the future because really, you weren't in a relationship, so really... did you break up? I've grown and realised, sometimes they're actually harder than real break ups. In a relationship, you knew what the relationship was and broke up because of it. But a situationship you never got that opportunity to have the relationship and fuck it up. You just get left wondering if it would have worked or not...

At the point I am writing this, I don't drink that much, and by that, I mean the occasional glass of wine... well, RARE glass of wine. I don't party any more and I don't belong to any social scene any more. I just do my own thing. I'd been through the druggy clubbing stages of life. Some would say a little too extreme. I'd lived overseas on my own in London for a year when I was just nineteen/twenty and saw a lot of dark shit. Went through a lot of dark shit. Been involved in a lot of dark shit. A lot of shit that people don't know, or if they know, I'd played a lot of it off in a humorous manner, but not one time did I really show how I was affected by it all. My life now compared to what it was in my very early twenties is a complete flip. All I cared about back then was where I was getting drugs from, what club we'd end up at, and who I was going home with that night. I was irresponsible but it was the life I was hooked on. It shaped a lot of who I'd become in the coming years.

But now, living back in Sydney, I like to work my boring corporate job that sucks the soul out of me, but I know I'm fucking brilliant at it. I like to go home and watch copious amounts of reality TV mixed with the occasional rom com without thinking it's lame, and I like to do it all on repeat until the weekend when I often go for coffee and drive to Kmart to spend money on things I really don't need. My life was completely different to what I was used to years prior, but the same thing that existed in both worlds was I was ready for someone, but no matter who I'd met... they weren't ready for me.

I guess what made me start writing this is the fact that I feel like I really have a story here to say and I think a lot of people would agree it's a fucked up construct about dating where being 'in a relationship' is almost like a death. So many of us find ourselves in situationship after situationship and they just don't seem to end up evolving. We're all constantly left wondering what if, and what we find is we keep adding to our own baggage of problems in our minds, but what's fucked is can we even have the right to call it relationship baggage if none of them were fucking relationships? What is everyone so scared of, yet wanting?

I've been an out homosexual half of my life. I came out quite young for the guys in my age group, only fifteen. It's not crazy young in today's world; however, I remember out of all of my friends, I was the first to tell my parents, of which back in 2008 when I did it, that was a huge deal within my friend group. It didn't go down well with my parents, well, my dad handled it a lot better, my mum didn't so much, but it got better, much better, and today they're two of my best friends who I really hope one day I get the joy of introducing them to someone I grow to care for just as much as them, but as time goes on I continue to doubt if that day will ever come. There's an aftermath with coming out to your parents that most gays have where they spend a couple of years really figuring out who the fuck they are in this world. I know now that I'm older, that that really doesn't ever change. We're all constantly trying to figure out who we are, but I think as a gay man, it's almost like a rite of passage that you finally open up and let out who you finally can be first, then move forward in life continuing to be open about yourself. I went through that REALLY young, at an age where you're kind of trying to do that anyway. For most 'in the closet' non-heterosexual people of that generation, they came out around eighteen to twenty-five, then followed their couple of years of figuring their 'different' selves out. But for me, I was processing being an angsty evil-to-my-parents little gay boy at fifteen and by maybe seventeen/eighteen I thought I'd gotten that all sorted.

Once I'd thought I'd gotten that sorted, I remember one by one my friends were coming out. I was there for them. I picked them up, took them out, drank, made them happy, and it was fun! I finally had people that could understand what I'd gone through years prior. But as they took their years from then on to figure themselves out, I felt like I was again, kind of ahead, since I'd already processed that part.

From an early age, I was ready for my Mr Whoever He Was. I didn't know where to find him, but I also grew up in the age of the apps, where your future fling, thing, lover, boyfriend, whoever, could be 1km, 5kms, 10kms, or overseas, but readily available at the press of a touch screen. Anything was possible then thanks to technology, but what was also possible thanks to it, was fucking it all up for everyone.

I had a boyfriend in my teen years, not long after coming out really, who at the time I thought was the love of my life. Oh, I was wrong. He was great, for my teen years at least. We went with it because we both really just liked each other. We said 'I love you' to each other. Whether we meant it properly... who knows, since we were teenagers, but it didn't last that long after saying it, BUT we did continue to see each other for a while because that part was good. But becoming an adult and dating other guys, I think it was then that I realised I was never really IN love with him, and that kind of... fucked up my sense of being able to identify what being in love really was.

What I don't want to do is sit here writing all of this, talking all *Sex and the City* at you with my *I couldn't help but wonder* thoughts every twenty pages. But I can take you down the path of how fucking confusing dating in the modern world can be with essentially, my dating life... lovers... things... flings... but never boyfriends or relationships.

Zeke

Probably, one of the first confusing things I've ever been stuck in was with who we'll call Zeke. We met in a dirty grotty club in the city, made out, I think, wait yeah we did. I was twenty or twenty-one. The music was blaring, really heavy bass dark electro music which I loved. I went to this club every single weekend, but I'd never seen Zeke there before, or at least never noticed him. He was stunning. Dark hair, dark eyes, olive skin, taller than me but not too tall. Good style, a smile that I could stare at forever, skinny, jackpot. We hung out the entire night dancing inside, running outside to hold hands and smoke cigarettes and just stare at each other whilst chatting and making out. For some reason, he made me sweat and my heart pitter patter… but also I was on ecstasy so it might have been that too. When it was time to go home, he begged me to stay out with him and keep clubbing (it was 5a.m.) but I said I couldn't because I had a family lunch the next day. Writing this now, I have no fucking idea how I survived that lunch. But we exchanged some form of social media, no idea which one, and planned to see each other again. Usually that means it won't happen or we'd leave it as a memory for that one night, but he actually followed through.

We met up maybe a week later for drinks at a dodgy bar in Newtown. It was the first night we both were actually in the moment, just us. The club was fun but all of our friends were there and staring at us, so finally, it was nice to hang out one on one. Chain smoking, drinking and talking about how fucked up our lives were yet laughing through the entire date. I was once again staring into his eyes and looking at that smile, this was going amazingly. He kept buying me drinks and putting his hand on my leg. We made out again later in the night. I don't know if it was the 3-4 hours of practice on the weekend or what, but this guy could really kiss. I know I'm a good kisser, but I remember thinking, *Jesus, this guy matches me so well.*

I remember looking at him thinking, *Holy fucking shit, this is one of the hottest guys, I've ever seen,* but I obviously couldn't say that to him because I'm trying so hard not to be a psycho.

We made out more, pretty much for the rest of the night and said we'd do drinks again. I got into a taxi and went home... to my parents' place because that's where I lived then (this was in my very early' twenties, probably twenty) and he slowly became someone I'd message every day and just talk absolute trash with. It was nice. By social media dating or whatever you'd call it, it was really nice, but it didn't go anywhere at the time.

Unfortunately, we disconnected as maybe two or three weeks later, he went through a really rough patch with his family. Nothing to do with coming out though. It was sad. I was sad, but I wasn't upset that nothing could happen from it because what happened, I entirely understood.

Someone died.

I won't go into it but it was heavy. So we disconnected

despite me saying I was there for him if he needed it. Selfishly, it was a massive shame as I'd met someone who was super sweet, super lovely, and one of the hottest guys, I'd ever pulled from a dirty make out in a club at 2a.m. We disconnected for a couple of years I think, but reconnected later down the track, I can't even remember how.

Oh wait, that's it! I ended up becoming really good friends and future flatmates with someone he was good friends with because... Sydney.

We reconnected through her, I don't even remember where we saw each other, but it just kind of happened. Next thing we went for drinks again, which didn't involve making out, but definitely included talking about how fucked our lives were and laughing through it. We were really good at that topic. Then, when finished with drinks, he walked me to the train station but as we're getting to the gates, he turned my body to face him, grabbed my face, hand on each cheek and kissed me on the lips. Not a make out, no tongue, but still enough of a kiss to make my heart skip and confuse the shit out of me for the entire train ride home. It was that little peck on the lips saying goodbye that made my brain go a million miles an hour. He handled me like I'd never thought I'd enjoy. Hand on each cheek, grabs my face, and almost doesn't give me a second to react before kissing me.

Did all those feelings from years prior come back? Absolutely. Did he still have those feelings? Who knows! I still to this day don't have a clue, but it was back. We were talking everyday again, seeing each other more and hanging out as friends... I thought.

I ended up living with the mutual friend not long after Zeke and I started to hang out again. She could see it. We would sit up late in our disgusting dingy terrace house so many nights discussing how Zeke was acting around me in comparison to how he was acting around her, or anyone else. I could feel it start to drive me insane. It was making my brain completely overthink every single text, but I also knew whenever my phone would light up with a new text message and his name showing, I'd smile. Fuck. We're fucked now.

It was getting so frequent that we would go for dinner or drinks, or even hang out at my house with or without friends. He'd hold my hand a lot and beg me to let him stay the night, and every chance he got to randomly kiss me he would. Never a make out, just a random peck. It was a head fuck.

It came around the time of our friend's birthday. She was having a birthday dinner at a nice restaurant. He came over to our house earlier on, asking just me if he could, not even our friend whose birthday it was. He was nervous so told me he wanted to go for a drink with just me beforehand. I told him, I had wine so we could just sit in the backyard. He ended up being late anyway, so it didn't really matter. We walked to the dinner, hand in hand, sat next to each other, his hand on my leg – his hand, my leg. Head. FUCK. It was making my head start overthinking literally whilst sitting right next to him. I just remember every time he lifted his hand to have a sip of his drink, I'd be thinking, *Put your fucking hand back on my leg and make my heart skip,* and he would. It was like a magnet was bringing my leg and his hand back together every time. It was making me feel really secure at that moment. I knew he was nervous beforehand, probably minor anxiety, but I wasn't sure why... unless it was for me?

Even when eating, I ordered some burger because I couldn't be bothered reading the menu and it was cheap, and when the waitress got to him, he just looked at me and went, "I'll just get the same as him," and smiled at me.

I thought it was fucking adorable. When the food came, he took his hand off my leg which I thought was FINE because he had to eat. But no, he took his hand off my leg for 1 minute to cut his burger into quarters so that he could eat it one handed and stick his hand back on my leg. I couldn't stop smiling. Probably one of the most stupid things to be gushy over a guy about, but when you're relatively new to dating and had one of the most attractive people right in front of you, you thought, wow, what a guy.

LOSER.

The dinner led to drinks back at the birthday girl and my house. Our house was filled with people, but Zeke just wanted to sit in my room, lie on my bed and watch me get changed for the party we were going to later on. Only leaving my room to get another drink or sit out the front and have a cigarette away from everyone. People came into my room to sit with us and chat, but I noticed they'd leave after 5 – 10 minutes. I didn't know why, but I felt fine being just with Zeke.

We eventually left to go to some random warehouse party that the birthday girl made us all get tickets to. Even in the taxi on the way there, he demanded I sat in the middle and him on the side, again, his hand glued to my leg, and one of my friends on the other side of me giving me eyes and continuously looking down at his hand on my leg and giving me a smirk. We got to the warehouse party. It was fun. I remember it being really fun... but also really intense. Zeke kept trying to drag me off to places, but I remember wanting to spend at least some of the night with the birthday girl or at least around her, since it was her night. He wasn't annoyed or being annoying, it was just fun and a lot of tension was slowly brewing.

It was in the early hours, maybe 1 or 2a.m., and I looked at Zeke and the birthday girl, they were suddenly on drugs. I was not and I didn't want to be, but immediately after realising they, and everyone else there, were on it, I just wasn't enjoying myself. It wasn't that I was jealous, it was just that I thought we were all having fun without it and suddenly realising we weren't all on the same level, it isn't that fun then. Later on, I turned to another friend (someone else we lived with) and just asked if she wanted to go home.

She turned to me and said, "I've been waiting hours for someone to ask me that... yes... let's get the fuck out of here," so we did.

I turned to Zeke and said, "I'm going," which followed with him yelling, "WHY?" at me like I'd just offended him.

"I'm exhausted and really just feel like crashing! It's 3.30a.m. in the morning, so don't act shocked!" I said back to him.

He gave me a huge cheeky smile, grabbing my face, kissing me and telling me, "Will I see you again? Can I stay with you?"

Of course, I said yes, despite the fact, I knew he'd be coming back to ours at like 6a.m…. dammit.

My other housemate and I got in a taxi and went home. We went straight out the back and sat and had some wine and a couple cheeky cigarettes. We often did that to finish the night with a little chat to recap the night we'd just had. We were talking about the birthday girl and how we both saw her having such a fun night until she put me on the spot and asked, "So, what's really going on with you and Zeke?"

I really didn't even know how to answer the question besides saying… "I don't really know, but it's nice."

"You literally looked like boyfriends tonight."

"Really?"

"YES! We were all talking about it at the dinner table."

"Who was?"

"Literally, everyone at the dinner. You two were so cute, but everyone also had a weird idea about it that it wasn't what it looked like."

"What does that even MEAN?"

"Well, from my perspective it just looked like two extremely close people based on lust and love for each other, but it was so couply it was adorable. But since everyone was talking about the fact you two weren't together too it made everyone kind of worried."

"Shit."

"Not that you have to be worried! It was just all of our observations."

"I still don't even know what that means but honestly neither of us have said we even like each other, it just feels automatically implied."

"That's not always a bad thing though… buuuut, sometimes it's important to at least say it."

"So, I should tell him I like him?"

"I think so! You two make sense! We were all at the table hyping you guys up! And at the party he literally couldn't take his eyes off of you."

"Fuck, OK, now, I'm nervous."

"Is he coming back here tonight?"

"I told him he could, yeah."

"Well, maybe in the morning bring it up?"

"Oh god, no, that's too real."

"Hahahahaha, that's true! But maybe real is good?"

That line stuck with me, even today, for the rest of my dating life. REAL IS GOOD. And I thought it was. What was so scary about being real with someone?

Well, we're going to find out, aren't we!

We both finished our cigarettes and wine and finally rolled our way to our bedrooms. Her with absolute bliss being able to go to sleep after a nice night out. Me, with the crippling anxiety of knowing Zeke was coming back to my bed to sleep over. I actually didn't even know if he meant in my bed or in the birthday girl's bed or even on the couch. All those thoughts going into my mind as I lay in bed wondering, *When the fuck is he coming?*

Hours went by, he'd texted a couple times asking if it was still OK to come over, each time me saying,

Yeah, stop texting me. Just call me when you're out the front, so I can peel my eyes open and open the door for you.

He finally turned up… probably 6a.m., dove into my bed in just his underwear, spooned me and we tried to fall asleep. He kissed the back of my neck, it was nice. Every single time it made my spine go all jelly. It was really nice. Then 'Grindr message sound' from his phone…

Again...

And again...

It kept going off the entire time we were trying to sleep, finally to the point where I rolled over, turned his phone on silent and went back. He kissed the back of my neck again and I was even more confused.

Obviously, I had the app as well. Every gay guy in Sydney has the app. But to hear it go off when you're in a sweet moment with the guy you like who doesn't really know you like him yet kind of obviously knows you like him is FUCKING AWKWARD.

I tried to make my brain shut off and fall asleep. It kind of worked.

I woke up at 11a.m. I was at an age where I could sleep until 3p.m. every day if I could, but I also lived in one of the busiest areas of the suburb so foot traffic outside my bedroom window often woke me up. Zeke was still dead asleep, rolled over away from me.

I got up, made coffee, cleaned a little from the party, since I thought it would be nice for the birthday girl to not have to worry about it so much. Had another coffee. Had a couple cigarettes despite definitely not needing any more, since I smoked half a pouch the night prior. By then it'd been an hour or so.

I checked on Zeke again. He looked so cute in my bed and tucked away with a grumpy face on. Definitely not happy in whatever dream he was in. My other flatmate came downstairs and we just talked on the couch for a bit. We heard the birthday girl and her friend in her room slowly waking up. I made a huge pot of coffee and went up. She was ecstatic to see me with coffee in my hands. She asked where Zeke ended up straight away after having a sip of coffee and a puff of her cigarette in bed. I was like:

"Dude, he's in my bed."

"Oh my god, really! He disappeared but obviously, he disappeared somewhere special! Tell me everything!"

"No, no, no, nothing like that, we just spooned."

"Well, the night wasn't that fun without you two."

"Wait, when did you guys even get home?"

"Maybe 4… 5?"

"Zeke didn't get here till like 6 – 6.30."

"Well, that doesn't make sense."

"Yeeeeeeah."

"Did he say where he was?"

"Something about the Imperial."

"Oh, then that's fine, we were there too!"

"Yeah, but did you even see him there?"

"Actually, no."

"Strange."

By this point, we'd been chatting for a while and it occurred to me that Zeke should probably get up. I went downstairs and into my bedroom just to check. He'd woken up and was just lying in bed on his phone.

"Hey!"

"Hi."

"Do you want some coffee?"

"Yes, please, but quick, I should really go."

"Why are you rushing off? You just woke up."

"I just want to go home."

"Why don't you come upstairs and hang out for a bit first?"

"Nah, I have to go."

"But it's your friend's birthday weekend still, it'd be nice to just say hi."

"Hmmm."

Zeke skulled his coffee pretty quickly. I could sense a mood. Probably, extremely hungover with very low serotonin levels. I didn't really want to be around his mood so I let him rush and gather his things in the frenzy he was in. He told me he was going upstairs to say goodbye. He never did. He peed, then left. I found it quite rude but whatever.

My friend, the birthday girl, wasn't impressed later on when she came downstairs and found out he'd bailed without even saying good morning or good bye or even asking how her night was considering he disappeared.

He called me later that night to thank me for letting him stay over and that he had a really nice time, specifically with me. It was then that the other flatmates' comments from the night before started sticking in my mind. *Real is good,* kept going over and over in my brain.

"You know I like you, right?"

"What?"

"You know I like you, right?"

"Umm."

"Fuck."

"Is... *ummmm*... well."

"Fuck."

"Look."

"No, did I just, forget it."

"You're like a brother to me."

"What?"

"You're like—"

"DON'T."

"Look, I really like you, but not like that."

"Yeah, I got that."

"Can I see you soon?"

"Sure!" – I died inside.

"OK, sorry, shit, OK, see you."

I hated myself.

I called an immediate conference with my housemates, both

of them, birthday girl and other, to go over the recent events. Everyone in the living room. NOW. I panicked. I told them both that I'd told Zeke that I liked him. What the fuck had I just done? Could I take it back? Was Zeke the one to lead me on or was I just reading an entire situation wrong?

No! I couldn't have been! His fucking hand was on my leg the whole dinner. He was literally eating a burger one-handed! He was staring at me the entire time at the party. Everyone at the dinner table thought we were a couple. He KISSED THE BACK OF MY NECK NONSTOP LAST NIGHT.

I was freaking out. The girls were as confused as I was. There was nothing else I could have done but ask the birthday girl to roll a joint and share three puffs with me, so I could make my brain jelly, so I could attempt to sleep through the night.

It worked. It was lovely. I couldn't feel my fingers. I slept perfect, alone in my bed, no kisses on the back of my neck, no Grindr notifications buzzing through the night. Oh god, is this making my brain jelly but also start remembering all the fucked-up things? No, no, back to sleep Morgan. Drift off, goodnight.

I woke to my alarm going off at 7.45a.m. It was Monday. Work time. At this time, I didn't have a corporate job. I worked in a fun photography studio with a bunch of eclectic people who appreciated my excessive swearing and the fact I was a young early twenty-something-year-old who acted like a thirty-year-old, well, I thought, but no I definitely was still acting like a young twenty-something-year-old.

I recapped to my boss the events and horror that had happened over the weekend. We had that kind of relationship. Big sister, little brother friendship. Jaz was this big fun loud woman with big platinum blonde curly hair that told me the second she realised I swore just as much as she did, she immediately knew I had to be a part of her team.

We talked for 10 minutes over the coffee machine and her mouth constantly gasped, going, "Noooo," and me going, "Wait... it gets weird," or, "Wait... it gets worse."

All of a sudden, we realised we got absolutely no work done. We sat at her desk talking about Zeke until lunch time. We both didn't give a shit that we got no work done, since the job was fun, easy, but also paid us really atrocious wages for the amount of bank we knew was rolling into the business.

I got a text in the afternoon from Zeke asking if we could hang out that night. I was still at the studio, when my phone went off. My jaw dropped. Jaz saw it and said, "Whaaaaat," and I simply picked up my phone and showed her the notification.

I was extremely confused. I showed the big sister boss and she was just like, "If you say yes, you're fired." I obviously said yes and told her I said no... but I followed the text up with a, *But are we OK?*

Yeah, of course, we're OK?

But, what I said.

I'm fine, are you?

I mean... it kind of feels shitty.

Why?

Because I thought you liked me back?

I do, as a friend.

That's not what made you kiss me randomly and spoon me though.

Can't friends do that?

I don't do that with my friends... and I know you don't do that with any of your other friends.

Well, I don't like you like that.

All right, I got it.

I didn't end up seeing Zeke that night. My housemate did though, the former birthday girl. I didn't know they were going to hang out. Thank god, it wasn't at the house.

My housemate got home and told me she was at dinner and asked why I didn't come. I told her, I didn't even get invited and she was confused as Zeke told her that I just didn't want to come. I told her I didn't know about dinner and that Zeke and I had spoken awkwardly but he said nothing about dinner and I didn't know she was going either.

Flatmate confusion.

We were both perplexed. Why tell one person the other didn't want to go to the dinner at all but then not tell the other where or when dinner was? Especially to say that to two people who FUCKING LIVE TOGETHER!

She told me a few things, like how he and I had spoken about liking each other, well, me liking him. She told him he acted like a dickhead. He told her he was seeing someone else and had been for about two months. She told him she wasn't impressed with how he'd been treating me. He acted confused but apparently she could see in his eyes that he knew he'd really fucked up.

I never spoke to Zeke again… properly.

A few months had passed. I was out at another dirty dark dingy club with my best friend Hunter, but not the same club I'd met Zeke in, don't worry.

Hunter and I both needed a night out, as shit in each of our lives had become a little chaotic, so we just fucking did it. She and I worked together but were best friends before even working together and luckily didn't work in the same direct team so we never had problems differentiating work and friendship. I should also clarify, this wasn't the same company as the fun studio. I, like most early-twenty-year-olds, had to have two jobs in order to pay for my life. I also worked at a fashion company within their Ecommerce studio and content team. I worked as a production runner rushing all the product through, and Hunter worked in the content team writing about all the shit product I was rushing to her.

She knew all about Zeke from the countless times we had cigarette breaks at work and nights where we'd go for a drink after work and just bitch about men.

The night at the club was fun, exactly what we both needed. Dancing and drinking and acting like dumb-fuck-idiots. Hunter was perfect for that. Just dancing and acting like absolute jokes of humans. Dancing the wave. The lawnmower, acting like fools but always smiling and laughing despite knowing people were looking at us like weirdos. That's best friends for you, I guess. Two people who simply will not judge each other, but also still judge the fuck out of you when you know it's needed. Hunter and I had it down.

All of a sudden, I saw Zeke in the corner of my eye.

The lawnmower dancing stopped. I didn't want to be seen looking like an idiot. I hadn't seen him since the morning after my housemate's birthday.

My heart sank into my throat. Throat? I don't know where my heart is meant to be but it's not in the right spot right now; I'm drunk, I'm not in the right spot right now! My brain's going a million miles an hour. Fuck.

He looked good. He looked really good. It killed me.

Hunter noticed my change of attitude. She knew I'd seen some sort of a ghost.

"Who is it?"

"You know who."

"Where the fuck is he?"

"No, Hunter."

"MORGAN! WHERE THE FUCK IS ZEKE?"

Hunter knew what he looked like from pictures and she'd met him once, but she couldn't spot him in the club since the lights were all fucked and dark still.

I walked away, going upstairs to another level and Hunter followed. It was quiet and I said, "I just think it's smarter to change floors for the moment. He'll pass. I'll pass. I just want to have fun."

We went and bought more drinks... and shots. We both looked at each other, Wet Pussy shots in hand and went 'To Us' and downed our shots and smiled and laughed. I needed that little moment to remember that I was there having a fun night with my best friend, not to worry about a guy I hadn't heard from or seen in months. As I turned to go down the hallway, bingo. There's Zeke looking at me and smiling. That fucking smile. Got me. Got me fucking good.

"Morgan!"

Oh no. I'm screwed. The feelings. I had to go down that hallway to go back to the dancefloor and the crowd of people were pushing me towards him.

"Hi."

"Morgan!"

"Hey, have a fun night." What the fuck was I saying? I wanted to tell him he was beautiful and grab his face and kiss him. *No Morgan, what the fuck, don't think that, you loser.*

I kept walking and passed him down the hall. He looked confused as to why I ignored him and brushed him off. All of a sudden, I felt a massive shove against my back and turned around quickly to realise Zeke had pushed Hunter into me... I was completely shocked. Little did I know in that second that Hunter had pushed him first. I saw Hunter launch at him and shove him against the wall of the hallway and yell, "LEAVE HIM ALONE!"

I was mortified. I grabbed Hunter and rushed her away from the situation and down the stairs to the original lawnmower, wave dancing floor. As I looked at Hunter, I realised... fuck... that was actually a really good thing she'd done for me.

He's going to hate me, but she's really looking out for me. She hugged me and went, "It wasn't going to happen. I did that as you need to move on and now he hates you so you can."

We immediately pissed ourselves laughing at what had just happened and skulled our drinks and ran off for a cigarette. We're giggling and then I saw Zeke come out to the smoking section. He saw me and immediately walked away. It worked. Hunter shoved him into a wall and Zeke wanted nothing to do with me. I was free. Hunter saved me from the most beautiful man I'd ever pulled in a dirty night club. Yay!

Zeke and I never spoke again… but thanks to social media, I knew he was in a loved up long-term relationship within three months after that night. Thanks, social media, really making us feel fucking great ONCE AGAIN! Can always count on you.

Jack

After Zeke, I didn't date anyone for a long time. I couldn't.

I definitely had people who were interested in me. I didn't want to date them though. There were a few guys who I'd slept with. Some were regular. Some definitely not. Actually now that I think of it, it wasn't a few. It was a lot.

I really didn't want to date anyone, but I just wanted to sleep with people and enjoy that for what it was. I did that for a while. Then, life led me to Jack. Jack was lovely. Messaged all the time. Would come over simply to spoon me. We'd been talking for years randomly over Facebook, after he'd sent me a random friend request. His picture was cute. Really obscure face but quite hot.

He wasn't my generic type being the basic as fuck tall dark and handsome, but I was still completely attracted to him. Blonde, blue eyes, pale skin, tattoos, a little bit chunky but in a good way, different to what I'd normally been attracted to. It was nice to realise my brain wasn't so finely wired to just the one type of man.

We'd actually been speaking for a long time. It'd been maybe two years of chatting then we realised we lived an 8-minute walk from each other. He'd been someone I'd talked to not long after I got back from London, but we'd never actually met. We just spoke online, which was always kind of nice to have someone who'd listen to you all day long. Kind of like a pen pal, however... we lived in the same city so now I'm thinking wow times were weird.

Of course, I invited him over to mine because I'm a greedy little shit who didn't like to move much. He came over the second we realised we had the ability to see each other within a 10-minute thought.

We watched *Gilmore Girls* (*I was depressed, OK?*) and talked for hours. I told him to stay the night and he did.

We spooned the entire night and kissed a little. I could tell he wanted more, but I just wasn't mentally in the right place for it, especially since... well... *Gilmore Girls*. He kissed good, not as good as Zeke, his lips were so soft, like pillows, which made me think, *Are these even his lips or did he pay for them?* I remember thinking that with his tongue literally in my mouth and giggling inside my mind but I couldn't let it out.

We'd wake up in the morning. Morning breath and shocking hair, but it was cute. It was really nice. We continued speaking all the time, cuddling when we could, but it wasn't more than that.

I got the vibe he wanted more. I gave him a little more once, but not all of it. I wasn't ready for that, despite us exchanging nude photos literally all the time.

It was always a little odd with Jack. Sure, I was sleeping with other people, but I had absolutely no connection and no substance with them. I had both of those things with Jack, but I didn't want to JUST sleep with him. I think he knew I wasn't OK to date, so he never pushed for more than what I could give him. I remember thinking that I wished we didn't have that connection or frankly anything in common so we could just fuck. But how SAD is that!

Jack was really nice. We still talk to this day but nowadays it's not so much about sex or anything, we mainly just like talking and keeping the banter going. I don't really know if anything could ever happen with Jack now, I mean we never had sex though, so there's always the wonder.

We always wanted to, but again, after Jack fizzled, he was in a long-term relationship within four months of us doing whatever it was we were doing. It didn't end up being 'the one' for him but if anything came out of it, it was nice to know that when he got into a long-term relationship, our friendship was still there.

We kept in contact, literally nonstop. Who knows. Maybe Jack's the dude. Maybe. Who the fuck knows for now though.

Who really knows ever? And how DO you know?

George

After many months of trying to move on from the 'heartbreak' of realising, the guy you liked and invested so much emotional time into didn't like you back (take a sip of your drink ladies). But also after talking to many guys on apps and drinking to forget, when if anything it just made you remember, I finally let a new guy I'd been speaking to, and even kind of liked, come over.

He was lovely. George was older, not TOO much older, but a solid ten years, meanwhile at the time, I would have been twenty-two, so now that I'm in my thirties thinking back at it, it did seem a bit odd. But then again, that could just be my brain as I'm usually not attracted to younger guys myself.

George fit the type I'd concocted in my brain. Tall, dark, handsome, but this time not skinny, a little bit thicker but not too thick, and a few muscles but definitely not a gym guy. Hairy in a good way. Trimmed beard. Beautiful brown eyes. Really beautiful eyes actually.

George was successful, had his own PR business, ran so many famous accounts and clients' lives. I always felt small compared to him whenever we spoke.

I was still working two jobs, one in a glorified fashion

cupboard with Hunter and the other in that photography studio with Jaz.

Whenever we spoke, he always had really big problems or projects going on with work and it was super interesting and I secretly loved hearing about all of it because in my head I was always thinking, *Shit, is that what I have to look forward to in ten years?*

It was almost aspirational. I felt small compared to George, but at the same time I looked up to him.

He was really caring, would hold my hand, kiss me gently and frequently too. He made me feel really special. I don't know what it was about me that even drew him to me. Actually, probably the nudes I'd send him all the time.

He was sleeping over at mine for maybe a week until he asked me to get breakfast with him one weekend. I was actually really excited.

It's funny that you can literally share a bed for ages with someone yet its tiny suggestions like that that make you go, *Fuck, I haven't even seen this guy outside of my house.* The thought just never crossed my mind. I guess I was already comfortable with him.

The couple of days leading up to breakfast, we spoke nonstop. I also panicked about how I was meant to dress and how I was meant to act.

He hadn't seen me in my normal form before. Just underwear and t-shirts, and sometimes neither. I planned my outfits every night until the morning of. Every one of them I'd hated because I looked so boring in my eyes. Boots, singlet, shorts. Morgan, come on dude. Get it together.

Also remembering little details that he told me like how one of his parents had battled cancer. Morgan... you're a smoker. But he kisses you a lot. He had to have noticed it. But he also said he had a problem with smokers. But I never thought about it until now.

Was that a hint for me to quit smoking? I was young, I would have never quit for a guy. Bitch, I'll only quit for myself.

OK, Morgan, stop thinking sassy, go to bed. George is coming to pick you up in the morning for fucking breakfast. Was this a date? Oh god, here kicks in the quivering anxiety. Was I anxious or was it excitement? I really had no idea.

I slept only a little that night as I was anxious... or excited... about... myself.

George arrived bang on the time he said he would. He was always extremely punctual, even for the area that I lived in seeing as you could just never get a bloody parking space.

I hopped in the car, immediately noticing how clean his car was. It was a black Golf, perfect condition, spotless inside. He said he'd had it for a few years but it still had the new car smell which I remember thinking was a little bit suspect. All I could think was thank god my car was three blocks away and that I lived in an impossible-to-park suburb so he couldn't see my dead grandma's champagne-coloured bomb of a car.

(Oh wait, she wasn't dead then. She is now. RIP.)

George looked good. Pale blue t-shirt that fits well. Shorts, nice sneakers. The smell of adult cologne. Fuck, I should have put cologne on. He looked like he'd freshly shaved. His hair looked styled but not too styled. Like he'd just gotten out of the shower and dried it but really I knew he'd stared at himself in the mirror for 20 minutes making sure every hair fell correctly.

We drove a couple blocks before I sensed George in a slight mood. Something just felt off. My brain started racing with ideas.

Did he immediately regret meeting me in the real world?
Do I smell? Do I smell like cigarettes?
Do I look bad in natural lighting?
Is my combo of black singlet, black boots and black shorts too boring and dull?

I couldn't stop my brain, so instead I just talked. Who the fuck knows what I was talking about. He probably thought I was extremely nervous since when we were in bed, I was so calm and quiet and gently spoken. I couldn't stop though.

Some would say I had extreme word vomit. I'd like to think of it now as full-on Cady Heron *Mean Girls* projectile verbal spew.

It didn't stop. He kept driving and nodding and letting out the very rare giggle.

He stopped me and went, "So, where are we actually going?"

Me, being in a panic, said, "What do you mean? Aren't we just getting to know each other? Do we have to have this conversation already, George?"

Shit.

You fucking dumbass. He's asking where we're going for fucking breakfast, you moron.

"No, Morgy, where are we getting breakfast?"

No giggle, full serious. Fuck. He didn't find it endearing. Shit. Also, don't call me, Morgy. You're not my family. I hated that.

"Oh! Sorry! Let's just drive down this street and find parking and let's walk and find somewhere?"

"OK."

Dead silence came over us. George parked the car. We got out of the car. We walked to the cafe, sat down, and looked at the menu. Still silent. The silence was making my brain go a million miles an hour yet at the same time only observe all the movements of 'getting out of the car,' 'still quiet,' 'sit down,' 'still quiet!' I tried making conversation about which food I seemed to like the most. Nothing. George seemed angry at something. I wasn't forcing him to be there. Why was he all of a sudden not wanting to be there.

This was his idea!

I was starting to feel self-conscious like he didn't want to be there at all. BUT AGAIN, IT WAS HIS IDEA. Whenever I started feeling self-conscious, it often led to me getting in a bad mood, so I was really trying to hold back from letting a little bit of the Scorpio inside of me out.

We ordered the same thing. Well, I ordered, he just said, "I'll have that too," since he was probably in a rush to get out of there. I ordered The Big Breakfast. Probably not the best thing to order on a first… date, but I wasn't actually paying attention to the items on the menu, so when the waitress came to take our order it was just the easiest thing to blurt out.

We ate and made very awkward small talk. I'd try to ask questions about him, you know, some that weren't related to work. I'd get really short answers back.

Oh, this was not going well.

Was it the boots/shorts/singlet combo? Was it me sweating, since it was summer and 37 degrees outside? Did I fuck up wearing boots on a 37-degree day?

YES. All of it is going through my brain. YES!

I ate really quickly. We both finished at the same time. He offered to drive me home and I said it was fine because the walk was only about 5 minutes from my house. I walked him to his car to be nice, but again it was silent.

He gave me a huge tight hug, which I remember finding really weird, since he didn't seem like he wanted a bar of me the entire time. He also kissed me on the cheek, which I found nice but also strange, since he'd always kiss me on the lips and hold my face and call me beautiful within the safety of my house.

It was so weird. My brain was thinking at such a rapid pace I simply couldn't stop it.

I walked home, blasting heavy loud rock music in my ears to try to drown out the voices in my head telling me I'd absolutely fucked it. The music was so loud that when I took the headphones out I could hear ringing in my ears. That helped drown some of the quiet voices though, so I didn't mind it.

I got home, went straight to my room. Sat on my bed and finally the voices stopped. Silence. Don't know what the trigger was. Maybe my bedroom was the safe spot for my mind to finally slow down and pause?

I checked my phone after just sitting there for 10 minutes calming down. I had a text from George.

I'm sorry, I was so off. It wasn't you. I could tell you were thinking that. I just like you so much that I'm trying not to let myself. Please don't be sad. We will speak soon.

...

...

...

How was I meant to respond to that? *We will speak soon? I'm trying not to let myself?*

Please don't be sad? What was that about? Was I meant to feel sad?

He really knew how to make my brain go super rapid. And then I realised I liked him more than I thought I did. I didn't respond. I thought it seemed like the kind of text you'd send someone to get something off their chests rather than opening discussion.

Then, I pondered around how much I liked George. Did I really have deep feelings for this guy or was it just the fact he's someone I felt I cared about? Was I just romanticising the entire thing? Absolutely. All of it. I liked this guy a lot. I couldn't stop that, but was I making him a bigger deal in my head and forgetting the reality of us... yep.

I didn't hear from George for a bit over a week. He was online on the apps during it, and I could see him looking at my profile, but no word.

He finally messaged me saying, *Cuddle?*

I, of course, replied with, *Yes, please.*

We cuddled that night, and some more. It was nice. It was exactly what I'd wanted. It felt unconditional. No not love, just super easy and simple. Like a real connection without having to say anything. That's the feeling I was addicted to. Connection without words.

He left before I woke up. I'm usually such a light sleeper I've never had that happen before. I'm the kind of sleeper that one little move and I'll be awake. One little noise outside and I'm awake. It truly sucks.

I checked my phone and just saw a text saying, *I left at 6.30a.m., I'll see you soon, baby.*

I never liked being called 'baby' but that time I really liked it. Probably because I'm romanticising and overthinking the entire thing, but I wanted him to call me baby again.

I went to work with the biggest smile on my face. Extra extra (yes two extras) strong coffee in hand. I walked into my fashion cupboard job and everyone saw the smile and immediately questioned what went on.

"You got laid."

"No."

"Yes, you did."

"OK, bingo, you win."

"Zeke?"

"No, it's George!"

"Oh shit, yep, it's George now."

"Fuck sake."

I felt like I spoke about George all day long because people just kept noticing me smile. Did I never smile? Was I stone cold and never opened my mouth to show my teeth? Actually, that's probably right.

The day went on and I didn't check my phone until I finished work. No texts from George. I could feel the voices start murmuring in the back of my head again. I drowned it out with more loud music. I left work, got home, nothing still. Hung out with my housemates, made dinner, shit, shaved, showered. Still nothing.

A couple days went by. Nothing. Was I meant to send the next text? I thought about it for the next few hours after the thought went into my head. I was really bad at playing these games with men.

I didn't like playing games. I just liked going with whatever was going on and staying in the real moment. I thought about what to text and the absolute best I could come up with was,

Hey! How are you?

Fuck that's bad. But it'll do.

Nothing.

I woke up the next day. Nothing.

I woke up two days later. Nothing.

I never heard from George again. For some reason, I wasn't crushed. Sending that boring text to him made the voices in my head stop. I think it was a sign that I always needed to try.

Sending that text was my final try with George, without knowing it was the finale. No, it's not me being stubborn and having to get the last word, although that's often a bad trait that I have.

But despite not hearing from him, I gave it a go. I tried. Final or not. I gave it a go and that's what counts. I always had fond thoughts of George. The way he treated me when one on one in bed was how I wanted to be treated at that stage of my life. I didn't find a guy who was like that for a long time. But then I also grew up a lot quicker around that age, possibly thanks to George.

I think I was realising I was a romantic. An over thinker. A worrier. A carer. But most importantly, I realised I wasn't someone who played games. I tried, but being real was more worth it to me.

After whatever it was with George, I thought it was important to simply focus on my work and my personal life. I tried not to use the apps for anything but what they're really used for. Sex.

I was killing it at work. I was really putting all my time and energy into pushing myself to work my way up at both my jobs. That… wouldn't happen, but if you know the corporate world, you know I tried. I ended up leaving the studio job and ended up working full-time at the glorified fashion cupboard. Why the fuck did I do that…

Don't worry, when I resigned from my boss Jaz, she agreed it was the best thing at the time. Little did I know the next day when I was at my other job, Jaz had resigned too.

Other than that, I'd moved houses into a new place. The girls knew I grew to not be happy in our dingy gross terrace house any more. The dynamic changed. The girls and I got moodier towards each other. I'm not exactly sure what the catalyst was that shifted it, but once it was identified I knew I should probably get out.

The new place I'd moved into was much nicer, with other friends I had to start fresh. This particular fresh start would not last long.

During the time living in this house, I wasn't that comfortable having guys over. My room was in the middle of the house and the girls I lived with were always home.

I simply couldn't sneak a random guy from an app through the whole house into my bedroom without them being noticed or making some sort of sound that the girls would hear.

I wasn't in a headspace to start seeing people anyway, so it just couldn't really happen in that house when the girls were home, which again, they always were.

There were a few instances where guys I'd been speaking to on the apps were almost desperate to come over. Probably because I'd teased them enough to the point where they were getting annoyed, I could never have them over, nor would I get off my fat ass to go to theirs because, scary.

There was one night, one housemate wasn't home. The other in her room next to mine but already dead asleep. It was my chance. Some guy who had been speaking to me for about three or four days was in town.

He was in the army or navy, something which intrigued me purely for the reasons of the body. He would definitely be fit. Me... not fit, but still definitely intrigued.

I had a chance, I took it. I told him to come over via the garage door at the back because the front door would wake up my housemate. In hindsight, a very strange and stupid request from me seeing as opening that garage door literally was so loud it woke everyone, even the neighbours up, but I still did it anyway.

We had a nice time, I guess. As you could imagine from

someone from the army, he was a little bit rougher than what I had had in the past. Respectful, but still not my cup of tea. I was kinda into it in the moment though. We went with it. Next thing it'd been an hour and I didn't realise the time was 2a.m. Fuck. OK, he's got to go.

I got him out of there through the garage again. Ran inside, showered, peed, and went to bed.

In the morning, I woke up to my housemate, we'll call her Aileen, in the kitchen making a pot of coffee.

"Morning, Morgan! Want some coffee?"

"Oh, yes *ploise.*"

We spoke like idiots to each other.

"How was your night? Did you stay up late?"

She knew.

"Umm like 2a.m.? Just chilled."

"Oh, yeah?"

She fucking knew.

"Did Nancy come home?"

"Ummm, I don't think so. I didn't hear her."

"Oh funny, because I heard the garage door open a couple times. I just assumed it was her."

"Weird."

Aileen poured me a second cup of coffee, since I scoffed the first one down quickly.

"Did you hear something in the roof last night?"

"Huh? No? Do we have possums?"

"Nah, definitely not possums, it was more thumping."

"Weird."

I walked outside to the backyard, sat down on the outdoor lounge and lit a cigarette. Aileen followed me outside and did the same. She knew. She was trying to get it out of me. She knows. I'm screwed. Leave it alone. Don't say anything.

"Oh, now that I think of it, it was definitely not the roof, maybe the wall."

"Oh?"

"Yeah. Banging up against the wall."

"Nah."

"Ah OK, just me."

...

"Oh, you mustn't have heard it, since it was you banging up against the wall with some loud footed man you snuck in through the garage door."

"Fucking hell, Aileen."

Aileen started laughing. This is exactly why I didn't have guys over. I was more of a private person when it came to men. I found it embarrassing. Why is she laughing! Stop!

"Fuck yes, Morgan! We've been waiting for you to bring someone over! I just didn't think you'd be a moaner."

"A MOANER?"

"Oh yeah, I heard it all."

"Fuck, OK, never bringing someone back here again."

"No, do whatever you want, seriously, I don't care but your other housemate might."

"Really?"

"Yeah, our last housemate would bring home the occasional guy and she always acted funny about it."

"Ugh, I don't want to deal with that."

"Well, you won't have to deal with it from me. I'm just happy you're human."

Aileen raised her coffee cup and winked at me.

I couldn't think about anything else for the whole day besides what Aileen had heard from her bedroom. Was I that loud? What even was the banging? I was so confused because I didn't even realise there even was banging.

I opened my app later that day to receive probably fifty+ messages from the army guy. I realised I didn't even know his name. Whoops. Fifty+ messages was a little strange. I checked them and it was essentially him begging to come back over. He wanted another round.

I was so mortified by the entire thing that I didn't want to do it again. It was good, but it wasn't that good. Wasn't worth another round that's for sure. I immediately was bored of it and didn't respond. It was what it was.

Then I thought maybe he was just into it so much seeing as he was only here for a short amount of time, being in the army, or navy. I still didn't want to meet him again…

After the army dude, I didn't want to meet anyone else for a while. I got my head back into work and just enjoyed my time with my new house, for the little time that it was.

I ended up moving out of that house only after living there for five months, but I took Aileen with me. The other housemate Nancy was a psycho, we'll just leave it at that.

Aileen slowly became my pseudo boyfriend. My grandfather figure. My better half and my worse half. Who needs a boyfriend when you have a housemate that will get you chicken nuggets for absolutely no reason.

Note: We didn't move so I could have sex with strangers. We moved because the other flatmate drove us insane, and to add a dramatic point, tried to throw a concrete ashtray at my head.

New House

Having a new house meant having a new start. A new look at everything. A new set of rules when Aileen and I never really made rules, we just lived the same and wanted to continue living the way we wanted to live. It worked for us.

We had different lives, but the way we wanted to enjoy our home was the same. In a weird sense, I was in a relationship with my house and my housemate. But I still wasn't getting the action I'd wanted.

The house was a few suburbs over from the last in a really leafy and floral area. It was a three bedroom house with a backyard, parking directly out the front, big enough for us and our friends to come over all the time. Also in a quieter area, which was nice to be able to sleep peacefully at night finally.

This move really opened my mind up again to the potential of dating. After Zeke, Jack and George's, little rendezvous, I didn't think about dating for a long time, but a new setting and a new home meant a new circle of homosexuals on all of the apps I have on my stupid phone.

I hopped onto them and noticed a few guys that were interesting.

For the next few months, I became uber-slut. I had guys over all the time. Aileen was never home as that was always my preference to never have to worry. I wasn't secretive so much about it, I just liked my privacy. Simple.

I couldn't even tell you over the course of those months how many guys had come over. I also realised then that my taste in guys was very all over the place. My usual type was the classic boring line of 'tall, dark and handsome,' but duh, that's everyone's taste isn't it?

If not that, then the other boring type-options were surfer boys with blue eyes, or guys who looked like they'd been to prison. There's like three boring types out there, but then all the rest of the types are more specific.

But anyway, I did my thing, and then came along a guy I'd like to refer to as Ryan.

Ryan

Ryan was nice. We spoke all the time online. He was kind of my type? Not tall, dark and handsome, but tattooed, not afraid to dye his hair a bunch of different colours, not too fit, taller than me though, but not too tall, and overall just a really sweet person.

He was never shy about giving me forty compliments a day, god knows what about, since we hadn't even met by this point.

We would literally speak all day long for the first couple weeks but for some reason when he'd ask for coffee and I'd say yes, there was never any follow through.

After maybe two months of talking, I finally just said, "Do you want to come over and cuddle?"

He rushed over that night at like 11.30. It was sporadic but we just went with it. We cuddled, made out a little bit, nothing further, I wasn't fully vibing it though... the kiss was...well... bad.

I went to work the next day and he continued to message me. I don't know why I wasn't vibing it? Sure, the kiss and making out wasn't great but other than that I just couldn't put my finger on it. Maybe, it's that I didn't put my finger on it? Nope. Don't relate this to sex Morgan, you're giving this guy a go.

We'd continue speaking for a while but nothing ever really came of it. I didn't feel the need to make it more than what it was. A nice conversation that would happen every day for months on end.

Ryan always wanted to see me but I felt bad always coming up with some excuse not to see him. I didn't want to see him. I'm not sure, even to this day, why at that time I just wasn't vibing it. The real reason would come later down the track, but at the time I just couldn't figure it out. I was, like a lot of fucked up people out there, often attracted to guys I thought I could fix. But the kiss was just not good...

Was it that I couldn't fix Ryan? Was there anything to even fix? I just couldn't figure it out but I also couldn't be bothered trying to figure it out.

It was what it was. Boring.

Don't get me wrong, it was lovely having someone interested in me, but maybe he showed too much interest. I wasn't finding him attractive any more and maybe that had something to do with it. Too keen? I was never this person. I was usually the one on the other side, obsessing over someone who's not that into me.

We stopped talking after a while. Probably more on my end. The conversation just became kind of stale.

A couple of months went by and Ryan told me that he had a new boyfriend. I was happy for him. Good for him. But, he was still messaging me. And why is he literally telling me of all people that he has a new boyfriend. It was just really strange.

I didn't know why, but I was simply friendly in return. Messaging back once in a while, I noticed the messages would be immediately returned when I wasn't jumping to message him back so quickly. It made me a little worried that I'd gotten to this guy a little more than I thought.

He continued to message me and it was really flirty. I looked at his profile on one of the apps to investigate. Yep, just like you'd thought. An open relationship.

I stopped messaging back for a couple weeks because I found it really awkward.

A new guy started messaging me. He was kind of cute, but not my type, but I was friendly and would reply anyway. His profile said single so I was in the clear. A few days of random banter but nothing flirty and then I looked at his profile again.

All of a sudden it said, "Open Relationship," as his relationship status.

It's not that I was against open relationships, but it was more that I didn't want one for myself and didn't want to like someone who was in one, because I wouldn't ever be the one they'd pick the monogamous relationship for.

And then the thought crossed my mind… wait, it couldn't be. Was this Ryan's boyfriend? Was this a weird plan?

I asked the newer guy, *Oh, so you're in an open relationship?*

Yep. Is that OK?

I mean, sure.

You sound hesitant.

Hey, if it works for you that's great!

You wouldn't be in one?

Just personally, no. I would find it really difficult.

Why's that?

I dunno, I'd probably get jealous and just not be comfortable with it.

Not probably. I know I'd be jealous. I have no shame in admitting that.

Ah OK, lucky my boyfriend's OK with it.

That's great.

You actually know him.

Oh?

Heart palpitations start.

Yeah! You used to speak a lot.

What's his name?

Ryan.

Lol, I thought you were going to say Ryan.

Oh, really?

Yep.

Is that a problem?

I'm just not interested in that way.

OK, but what about if it was me in the room?

OK bye.

Really?

The conversation ended there. I didn't want to be a part of this any more. Ryan had gone to the extent to get his boyfriend to try to get me involved in us hooking up. It was an extreme measure. Quite impressive. Quite desperate. Yuck.

Ryan messaged me a couple days later simply saying, *So you're not into my boyfriend?*

I left it a couple days then just followed up with.

No, but because I'm not into people with boyfriends.

Simple. Easy. Respectful. Or so I thought.

But you weren't into me without one?

Ryan, do we have to do this when you have a boyfriend?

I just want to know if you were ever into me.

I was. But now that you have a boyfriend I'm not.

So if I didn't have a boyfriend would you be?

I don't know Ryan, but this is all a bit weird now.

I'll break up with him for you.

Ryan, please don't do that.

I will.

Ryan!

Ryan would continue to message me asking if he should

break up with his boyfriend for probably another month. I never responded. It was extremely manipulative as well as I wasn't comfortable with him ending a relationship for me when I didn't really want one with him.

Six weeks after we spoke, I found out he broke up with him, but it was via the boyfriend that I found out.

The boyfriend, well, ex now, told me I could have him. I said, *What happened?*

You really got to him.

What?

He's obsessed with you.

That's a bit scary.

I wouldn't be scared, but whenever we'd be looking for a third for the night he always suggested you and would get me to try to speak to you even after we'd spoken and you clearly weren't interested. It went on for ages. He started to creep me out a bit with it all.

That's just all a little too much for me.

I think the only way for him to move on would be for you to fuck him.

But I don't want to do that.

Or take him on a date?

I don't really want to do that either.

Well, he won't stop trying.

Did you two break up because of me?

Well, you were a contributing factor, but not entirely your fault, plus knowing your views on it all I could never blame you. It's all him.

OK, that's good to know from your side but I am sorry.

Don't be sorry. You had literally nothing to do with it all. None of it is really your problem.

OK.

Well take care, I just thought you should know all of this.

No, thank you for telling me.

No problem.

Something told me the story about Ryan then wouldn't be over. And it wasn't, but it was for that point of time.

***

A few months go on, I continued doing my thing, flirting and meeting with men who I wasn't interested in enough to pursue anything with. A few men were good to keep around for shorter periods of time, but no one that made my heart pitter patter the way I needed it to in order to feel like anything was worth more.

I was having a lot of sex. At that time with maybe three men on rotation. It was great for the next while, but I knew it couldn't go forever. Either someone would get feelings or just move onto their next person, but I didn't feel any kind of attachment to any of them. It's like we were free to go off and do what we wanted. I didn't miss anyone when there was any time apart.

I felt I was kind of getting to a very cold hearted point in my mind. I didn't value any of these guys. It's not that I wasn't attracted to any of them, I was definitely attracted to them enough to sleep with them. But I realised I didn't get the heart pitter patter feeling that I was craving. Sure, sleeping with someone you sometimes have it in the moment, but you have it just in that moment. Then when it's back to just texting, it's gone. Nothing.

I was beginning to miss the butterflies. That feeling in your stomach where you got knots. That feeling when the guy you liked texted you and you smiled. I realised I hadn't actually liked someone in a really long time.

Then along came a guy, who I immediately saw as a red flag. I was attracted to him enough to sleep with him, but he wasn't my type at all (or more so what I wanted my type to be). Short (my height, sue me), stumpy, definitely depressed as he didn't present himself in a way that he cared about his appearance in any fucking light. He would have been a mission for me to fix so I knew not to bother with that. I was attracted to him enough to sleep with him but I knew I couldn't date him. Let's call this one, Damien.

Damien

Damien should have been a massive, MASSIVE red flag to me from the get go. Was he at first introduction? Nope, but he should have been.

Damien was someone who would regularly come over... for the deed. Sex. Really. Fucking. Good. Sex.

Sex that I don't think I'd ever had with someone. Passionate and attentive, he knew exactly what I liked and I knew exactly what he liked, from experiencing not even from communicating. I don't know how, we just knew exactly what to do with each other and how each other liked it.

The only rational thought I had when it came to it was that I had that connection I'd been craving from someone, but this was solely sexual. There was a connection during the sex that was so passionate and crazy it became addictive. When we weren't having sex it wasn't there at all, but when we were it was uncontrollable. I'd never had this before.

It might have been the moans...

But it was becoming a habit of him coming over maybe twice a week for a while. It was always a solid hour or two of him being over. At first he'd come over, we'd talk for about 10-20 minutes, get down to it, then talk for 10 minutes afterwards and sayonara.

After a few months, it turned into hanging out in bed for another hour just chatting and getting to know each other. I didn't even notice until around this time that I was sleeping with only him. The other guys I'd had on my rotation I had made up excuses to not see because I was addicted to the excitement that was sex with Damien.

Did I want to pursue anything with Damien even though by then I'd gotten to know him so well? Nope. Still didn't feel those flutters, but his company was becoming more and more valued.

I couldn't say the same from his side though. He started getting more flirty and clingy, which was making me start to wonder if this needed to simmer.

I didn't let it simmer. The sex was just that addictive that I couldn't let it simmer. I was into it more than I was into the idea of anyone else. Even if the man of my dreams came knocking on the door begging for my hand in marriage, my brain would be like… *but sex with Damien!*

We continued doing our thing for maybe six months but during these six months there was never a question of a date or staying over. It just was what it was. The ideal situation for someone like me who definitely wasn't looking to actually date someone at that time.

Damien became my go to – I wasn't sleeping with anyone else. We were in sync with each other. Available when we could but unavailable at the same time. It was the perfect arrangement for me.

I think I started becoming more busy with work though as I didn't even notice that the days had become once a week. I'd get home from work exhausted and not wanting to have sex, so organically it just shifted. He said he understood but I could tell from his tone of voice that he was still annoyed. It was just known between the two of us that we wanted each other all the time, but it was also known on my side that he wanted more.

After a while, it became once a fortnight, then less. It was as if my side of the addiction had become numb. I didn't even realise or question it to be honest. Eventually the conversation stopped. We weren't sleeping with each other any more but I didn't really notice. My addiction to the sex with him had become blocked by reality. I couldn't arrange a time to get my fix because I was just too preoccupied elsewhere.

A while later, he'd messaged me saying, *I'm sorry, I've not been able to see you lately.*

That's fine, I've been so busy with work, I didn't really notice.

Oh, thanks.

No not in that way, I've just been pigeonholed into work and sleep.

That's OK, but I miss you.

Aww we should hang again soon.

I can't.

Haha, OK but why?

Because I've started seeing someone, but I still have feelings for you.

All of a sudden my brain was kind of relieved. I realised when I'd just suggested hanging out again soon that I probably wasn't going to even do that. I actually was genuinely happy for the guy that he was seeing someone. The connection we had during sex was something he should share with someone who cared about him when not just having sex. I knew I wasn't the guy for him, but was I using him? I thought we were using each other!

That's great you're seeing someone!

You're OK with that?

Why wouldn't I be? I want you to be happy.

You're not jealous?

No? Why? Should I be?

I guess I meant nothing to you.

What?

I wanted to date you but it just never went there.

Well this is also the first I'm hearing this.

I know...

...
...
... OK annoying.

Why did you never say anything?

I don't know. We just had a good thing going and I didn't want to ruin it.

It wouldn't have ruined it, it may have helped navigate it a bit better.

OK, but now that you know...

What?

Now that you know, does that change anything?

Well, now you have a boyfriend, so I can't feel any type of way besides that.

But if I didn't have a boyfriend?

But you do. I don't want to date anyone. I think it's great that you have a boyfriend.

OK.

All of a sudden this was really triggering to me. I'd just gone through this kind of shit with Ryan. I fucking hoped he wasn't trying to manipulate me into being his side piece or anything. I was respectful to someone when they got into a relationship. Good for them! I knew at the time I didn't want one, but I was still happy for them.

Damien and I didn't speak again for a long long long time. My brain didn't actually think about him. I did care about his well-being and happiness, but there was a comfort in knowing someone else was giving him what he desired. I wasn't upset that it wasn't me because deep down I think I always knew I couldn't give him that. I just immediately thought, *OK, well, I guess I have to find someone new.*

Awful I know, but I was still in my early to mid' twenties. Young and stupid.

Damien's not over quite yet, but for now in the story, he was.

Over the next few months, I don't think I really spent any time bothering with new men.

I was focussed on work again – not because it was going anywhere good, but because it was driving me insane. Overworked, underpaid, and hoping for a promotion that was never ever going to come.

Eventually, I gave up – quit my job at the fashion cupboard and focussed on my mental health because I'd shed enough tears and anger over a job that didn't work for me any more. I'd worked enough for them. This allowed me the time to go back to being the slut I needed to be to get a little bit of happiness back into my life (no pun intended).

I didn't meet anyone that really grabbed my attention, but my bedroom door became a revolving door for men. Some my age, some a bit older, some a lot older. Some returned, some only came for one visit. I didn't care. I was happy. Or was I?

Was I actually just trying to convince myself that if I kept having this temporary happiness of men a few times a week that it would be enough to say that I'm happy? I think now that I'm older that's exactly what I was doing. Not allowing too much time to actually let any thought take over my mind, but give myself a little bit of fake happiness to blend it all into an average, *Yeah, I'm happy,* state of mind.

After a couple of months of doing that and a combination of nightly job hunting, I eventually, got a job working in magazines. A bit of a dream at the time, I think a lot of people glamorised working in publishing but the reality was it was literally just another office job sitting at a desk, but I loved it. I really loved this job, probably the most out of any job I'd had so far. It was fun and creative and the people were fucking bat shit crazy and eccentric. A bunch of absolute kooks, so I felt like I fit in.

I was working my ass off and my bosses were really happy with me. I was killing it at this job to the point where I could say and do whatever I wanted because they had full faith in me as an employee.

Once I'd gotten to that point and was comfortable, I remember thinking I might be open to sleeping around again and having a bit of fun.

Then... I met Andrew.

Andrew

I'm going to pre-emptively say that Andrew is going to be a larger chapter than most. Andrew was amazing. I hope if he ever read this he wouldn't be upset. But it is what it is.

Andrew had messaged me on another hook up, dating, whatever the fuck you want to call it, APP.

But the conversation didn't feel… just sexual. We got along, in a way I hadn't really before with someone via a phone message.

He seemed to get my sense of humour pretty quickly. He also liked that I was really direct with him, something a lot of guys weren't comfortable with.

I've always been pretty direct with my feelings when it comes to the beginnings of something. Saying what I want up front. Saying what I don't want. And saying what I and they could expect out of it. Always being a little vague leaving the options open for potentially more if it felt right, but still being direct.

Whenever someone says the classic line of, "What are you

looking for?" I always answered with something along the lines of, "You can't expect everything or anything too much from these apps, so whatever comes, comes."

Most found it insightful because really... it was true. Some found it immediately annoying because I didn't respond with 'Sex' or 'Dates' or whatever THEY wanted me to say. But I said it every time because I believed it to be true. If sex was on the table, sex was on the table. If dates were, then yeah maybe try swoon me into going out on one, you might just get it. I was really just mentally open to whatever the outcome was.

Andrew loved the response because it was real and even said something along the lines of, "Fuck, it's nice to actually speak to someone who's realistic about these apps."

That got me in the feels. He got me... in the feels.

We didn't stop talking.

For maybe two weeks, we spoke all day every day, and would keep each other awake at night because we just couldn't go to bed yet. We had to know what the other said.

I felt chemistry. Something I hadn't felt in a long time.

There came a day when Aileen told me she was going out for the whole weekend. I didn't think anything of it besides me sitting out the back in the inflatable pool doused in tanning oil perfecting my tan lines but when the day came I thought... maybe Andrew would like to work on his tan?

(LIES I WAS HORNY)

I messaged him and invited him over, telling him I'd be home alone all weekend.

He immediately said, *Address and when?*

I said, *Whenever you want and here's my address*, and gave him the address.

He literally jumped straight into an uber and came over which I found even cuter, as if he was waiting for me to ask him to do something.

He came over. We hung out in the backyard.

I think he was a little shocked as I was smoking a cigarette but I didn't think anything of it.

Next minute, we're making out on the cold concrete. I'm sweating because of the tanning oil and the sun. I'm also already in just underwear as I'd been tanning.

It was hot. Really hot. Not just the weather, but the whole scene.

We calmed down for the minute, kept speaking, I dipped into the pool to cool down. He stripped into just his underwear and sat in the pool with me. 3 minutes later we're making out again… nonstop for half an hour. It was insane, I felt the electricity between us. I don't know where the hell this guy had been.

We were barely breathing; we were both so into it.

Of course I got up, held his hand and brought him towards my bedroom where we jumped into bed and continued making out. We eventually got sexual and without going into details (because my family could eventually read this part if they get to it) we were at it for hours.

Eventually, we finished. Laid there, exhausted, entwined, drenched in sweat.

I'd never had this with someone before. We just lay there for two more hours chatting and laughing.

It was amazing. I hadn't had this with someone in so long. I felt really happy.

Andrew didn't stay the night. He eventually went home but that didn't mean the conversation ended there.

He messaged me when he got home and said, *I really like your company that was amazing.*

I replied with, *Without sounding funny, that didn't feel like JUST sex to me.*

I couldn't agree more. There's a connection.

Oh, thank god, you feel it too and I'm not crazy.

No, I definitely felt it but what are we going to do about it?

I think we should just see where it takes us.

I like that idea. Go with the flow.

Exactly, without sounding cheesy.

Haha.

Simple. Direct. Easy.

I think I've also forgotten to mention that Andrew is a good ten years older than me. This wasn't an issue on either of our ends. I was twenty-four, him thirty-four (I think), this to me was kind of perfect as twenty-four year olds were never even open to the idea of anything potentially stemming into a relationship. We just weren't. Myself included. But I was more open than most. And Andrew was the first guy in a while that made me feel like opening my mind up to the possibility again.

Andrew had come over a couple more times, hung out, so much fun, nonstop laughter.

He eventually asked me on a date,

"What are we going to do though?"

"It's a surprise."

"Oh god, you should know about me now that I don't like surprises."

"Tough."

"ANDREW!"

"Nope, tough, you'll enjoy yourself though."

"But how do I know what to even wear?"

"Just dress comfy, maybe sports shoes."

"SPORTS SHOES?"

"Trust me, it's not sport, but it's something different that I've always wanted to do."

"OK, OK, I'm just going to go with it."

The day came around. I met him at my local train station and off we went.

At this point, I absolutely hated the new train opal card system because the whole tap on tap off thing didn't allow me to even know the final destination. I just had to go with it and be patient.

We got off at Circular Quay – right in the city.

We started walking, I'm wondering what the hell it was

going to be the entire time, him talking about his family dramas and laughing, obviously trying to distract me from the fact I didn't know where I was even walking.

We kept walking – me thinking, *this walk is going on for a while*. We're even walking in a direction I wasn't familiar with.

We turn a corner... there it is. It screamed at me.

"YOU'RE TAKING ME ON THE BRIDGE CLIMB?"

For those reading who don't know what the Bridge Climb is, it literally says what it is in the name. The Sydney Harbour Bridge... Climb. You climb it. It's possibly the most touristy thing in all of Sydney that I'd never done.

I was randomly so excited. My parents and my brother did it when I was really little and I was always so jealous they got to do it to the point when I grew up I was angry they didn't wait another two years for me to be able to go with them (there was an age minimum). Obviously, I didn't hold onto it forever, but when you're that little... yep, you hold a grudge.

"Yep! Isn't that a fun idea?"

"Oh my god, I just never would have thought of this."

"But will you do it with me?"

"Fuck yes!"

I was so excited, I think he was too because I was reacting so enthusiastically to it.

But when we got closer to the entrance my brain went, MORGAN. THIS IS A DATE. YOUR FIRST DATE WITH HIM IS THE BRIDGE CLIMB.

And I thought... *Oh, wow, if this works out our first ever date will be the Sydney Harbour Bridge Climb... forever. Wow.*

I got nervous. Not because of the heights, but because it was our first date. My brain just kept telling me to go with it. So I did.

We waited and finally got changed into our huge ugly grey jumpsuits and belts. We were being led out to the bridge exterior. I was in front, trying to listen to the history of the bridge but also just not caring because the inner child in me just wanted to get to the good bit where you're literally ON THE HARBOUR BRIDGE.

Every time the group would stop and the instructor would teach us more about the history, Andrew would come right up behind me and hug me from behind or hold my hips or something really cute. I wasn't used to this. Plus, my inner child was just screaming at me to have fun.

I just kept thinking, *Just go with it, stop overthinking.*

It's not that I was uncomfortable, it's just that I wasn't used to this kind of behaviour. I'd never been treated nicely like this. Yeah maybe a dinner or coffee, but something big like this had never come my way.

We were finally getting to the fun part of the bridge. The instructor let us go up the bridge separately. My inner child took over. I ran. I got yelled at because YOU'RE NOT ALLOWED TO RUN UP THE HARBOUR BRIDGE (due to safety), but I didn't care. I loved it. It was an adrenaline rush.

The only problem was, I literally forgot at that point that I was on a date. I was meant to turn around and do it with Andrew and for it to be an experience together!

Whoops.

We got to the top, it was so amazing up there. The whole of Sydney with a man's arms wrapped around me. It should have felt beautiful and amazing. It kind of did? I was still not used to this kind of treatment.

They make you take a photo when you're at the top. AWKWARD.

The instructor and photographer asked, "How do you two know each other."

I awkwardly said, "Friends!" with a huge smile.

I don't know if that was OK to say but what the hell are you meant to say plus I've had it embedded into my brain from fucked-up dates and 'things' with men that if you're not officially dating or boyfriends, you're really just friends. I also didn't want to say 'this is our first date' and have those looks come my way. 'Friends,' just came out of my mouth. I heard Andrew mumble a little *mhmmm,* but it didn't really click in my brain.

We took the picture, it was cute, but a bit awkward. We continued on with the bridge climb tour.

The way down wasn't as fun, probably because it was ending. Andrew kept being adorable and holding me every chance he could. Holding my hand whenever we'd pause to learn more about the history.

My brain was screaming. I wasn't used to this kind of treatment at all. I was only twenty-four and thinking, *wtf is going on?* But then, I kept remembering JUST GO WITH IT and I would.

We ended the bridge climb, went for dinner, it was really cute. Got the train home, he walked me back to my house and I went inside. He didn't come in. My flatmates were all home and their boyfriends and friends were all over.

The second I went inside, they knew I'd been up to something. I sat with them all in the backyard and lit a cigarette and Aileen took one look at me and went, "Where the fuck have you been and why are you so smiley?"

Everyone looked at me. All six people's eyes looking at me

"I... did something a little wild today."

"What?"

"… I… went and did the Harbour Bridge Climb."

"WHAT THE FUCK MORGAN."

"What?"

"That's just so out of character."

"Well… I wasn't alone."

"OH MY GOD, KEEP TALKING."

"… well it was a date. A first date. I've kind of been seeing someone I guess?"

Everyone didn't know how to take it all. They were all just in full disbelief because of my past and how closed off I really was (when I didn't think I was that closed off).

We went on debriefing the whole day. Everyone was shocked but excited and definitely getting ahead of themselves yelling that I had a boyfriend when I kept being defensive saying, "No, stop it."

Andrew and I kept seeing each other a lot. Like, more than I was used to with any man. We spoke all day every day. We started getting more and more involved in each other's past and histories and learning about each other.

About a month or six weeks had passed. He wanted to spend the weekend with me but his housemate was home. My housemates were also home, but he wanted a weekend with just the two of us.

Without really planning, he booked a hotel room. I thought it was exciting. I drove and picked him up and we went to the hotel.

The hotel was nice… kind of standard. Nothing special.

We went out and had dinner, went back to the hotel room and… well… you know.

ETC (trying to be PG here) (not sure why all of a sudden I'm being PG).

But then we really got deep diving in deep conversation.

He was talking about his housemate and how he wanted him to move out but didn't know how to bring it up. I was advising what I would do in this situation, especially, because I'd lived with so many housemates even by that point in time.

The conversation went for about 20 minutes, I think, but towards the end I pieced more and more details together.

The flatmate wasn't just his flatmate. The flatmate was his EX-BOYFRIEND.

I knew he and his ex-boyfriend had broken up maybe five or

six months prior to us even talking, but I wasn't aware that he and his ex-boyfriend still lived together.

A lot of information was flashing in front of me. I'd never been inside his house, only ever picked him up from out the front. He'd only ever come to mine and stayed the night. It was like a puzzle I was putting together but I never signed up for this puzzle.

Why couldn't he just tell me his housemate was his ex? Why was that a secret?

I was direct, as I always tried to be and asked him.

He said, he didn't think about naming him that as he didn't want me to freak out. I said, it's not made me freak out, but it would have been nice to have been told rather than piece it all together myself and have to ask.

We finished the conversation and ended up watching TV for a bit.

A couple hours of cuddling and giggling at the TV on the couch he turned to me and said, "I have something to ask you."

"Yeah, what."

"Well, a couple of things."

"OK, go."

"Well firstly, what are we going to do about dessert?"

"I'm not really hungry any more."

"Well, shit cos I am."

"What's the other thing?"

"Well... I was wondering... do you want to be my boyfriend?"

I froze. I didn't know how to answer the question. My brain was immediately saying things like, *Oh my god, Morgan, you've been waiting for this moment for ages. But is he ready? He still lives with his ex and you just found that out a couple of hours ago. What the fuck!* It all just kept playing on my mind because I knew I wasn't that comfortable with that scenario alone.

"I'm not sure yet."

"What?"

"Don't get me wrong, I do see us going in that direction, but I don't think you're as ready to call me that as you think you are. You still live with your ex. I'm not saying kick him out but how do you expect me to be comfortable with that when the ex is in the next room?"

Andrew, visually started looking super upset.

I grabbed his face, looked him in the eyes and said, "I know your brain right now is hearing me say no, I'm not saying no entirely. I'm saying figure out your shit and the answer will be a definite yes, but for right now, I'm not comfortable with the situation you're in and how I'd have to just deal with it."

He still looked sad, but not as sad once I'd said that. He understood. He said he still felt rejected, but that it wasn't a direct rejection, it was an understandable rejection.

I felt horrible for saying it, but I had to. I wasn't comfortable saying yes at that given moment but then again I thought, he wasn't going to tell me he even lived with his ex. If I didn't figure that out only a moment prior, I wouldn't have known, so would I have said yes?

Was I searching for something to say no to a relationship with Andrew? This man was the best man that had ever come my way in a long time and I was thinking I wanted this.

My brain kept saying go with the flow go with the flow. I tried.

After that, we kept seeing each other. It was really great. It was lovely, but some cracks started to form.

We weren't seeing anyone else, no apps, we'd agreed on that, but the question of a relationship wasn't resurfacing.

Andrew had moved out, found his own place and we were hanging out all the time.

He'd do little things like send me flowers to my office and

wait for me to receive them. He was a romantic. I was NOT used to this. I didn't think it was cute. I thought it was really cringe, but I went along with it, because it made him happy.

Valentine's Day came around and flowers turned up at my work again with a note saying, *Excited to see you tonight.*

We had plans to just do dinner and hang out. It was the first time in my life, I'd ever had a Valentine. I didn't know what to expect.

I got to his house, he'd prepared me dinner, nothing special just fish and chips and salad. Still yum. I was twenty-five, I thought it was chef's kiss.

I asked if I could have a drink but as a young person, I asked whilst I was already in the motion of going and getting one, and as I opened the fridge, I heard him go, "NOOO," but I opened it.

There was a rose. In the fridge. Chilling. Waiting for him to pick it out and present it to me.

My eyes opened and I grabbed the drink I wanted and shut it and pretended I didn't see anything. He came over and went, "I know you saw it," took it out of the fridge and gave it to me and gave me a huge kiss.

I was being swooned. I hated it. It was too cheesy but JUST FUCKING GO WITH IT.

We had dinner, he was romantic AS FUCK. I pretended to not be uncomfortable.

We just went to bed that night. Fucked. And went to sleep.

Over the course of the next couple of months, the relationship or situationship or whatever the fuck it was would slowly unravel.

He always told me that he was OK with the age difference. I was totally fine with his age gap, but I would learn soon enough that he wasn't with mine.

He would bring things up to me like, "Why aren't you thinking about this part of your future," and I'd simply say, "I'm twenty five, that is not even a factor in my life yet." Talking about children and buying homes and meeting the parents (that parent part I also know that's normal but it was a sign to me I wasn't there yet).

Andrew had a relative suddenly pass away come April.

I tried to be supportive and give him the space he needed to get through the hard times I knew were coming. One thing about me is I'd been through a lot of death even at the young age of twenty-five. I'd attended more funerals than weddings, so I knew some people needed space and time to mentally get through it.

I barely heard from Andrew and when I'd receive a call or message, I found it quite cold.

I just kept saying, "Just go with it," but it was getting to about two or three weeks that I'd been treated not badly I'll say, but pushed to the side.

He finally said, "Come over," after I'd said I wanted to see him."

I walked in, he was immediately distant. Not kissing me on arrival, an awkward hug. I sat with him on the couch, we spoke for a little bit, and I checked in on him. That was my priority, to make sure he was OK. I went in to hug him on the couch and he went, "I CAN'T DO THIS." He thought I was leaning in to initiate sex or a romantic connection. I leant back and went, "What? You can't hug me?"

Little did I know in that second, he meant he couldn't do THIS with me any more.

He went on to say literally that, "I can't do this any more." I was confused.

He belittled our entire situation saying, "We're just fucking and we're just aimlessly seeing each other," completely down playing the entire six months we'd been doing whatever it was we were doing.

I sat there and let him get it all out. This was something I know is a problem on my end. Just sitting there and taking it. Never speaking up.

He said he wanted us to stay friends, since that was what we'd been doing (fuck you) and I didn't say anything.

He turned on the TV. We're sitting three metres apart awkwardly. He put something funny on but neither of us were laughing. I gave it five minutes until the discomfort took over. I got up, grabbed my bag and walked towards the door.

He went, "What, you're leaving? You're just leaving me?"

I said, "I can't just sit here and pretend like I'm fine with everything you just said. Sort your shit out. I was just trying to be supportive," and walked out the door, not slamming it, but just closing it.

I got in my car and drove home. I felt numb.

I'd just been dumped and belittled to rethink everything I'd been through with this person. I didn't know what had just happened. I parked outside of my apartment, didn't even go inside, and walked to get cigarettes constantly checking my phone hoping he would call or text to say he'd fucked up. He didn't.

Call me selfish for feeling this way when he's dealing with someone passing but my brain couldn't think about his perspective any more. I'd been worried about him for weeks and he made me feel like the size of an ant. Like it was all just a waste of time.

I knew it was potentially just the sadness taking over his mind and him lashing out at me because he was obviously confused as well, but again, my mind couldn't see outside what he'd just said to me and made me feel.

I got cigarettes and sat out the front of the house on the front steps chain smoking for two hours. I couldn't bear to go inside.

Aileen came out for a cigarette and found me. I didn't speak.

She knew.

She sat next to me and just did that. Sat with me. I was numb.

I realised over the coming days, I was falling for this man. I have a habit never realising things when they are happening but I realised it later on.

I heard from Andrew a few days later. A text message where he essentially just reiterated everything he'd already said. Belittling the situationship, making me feel like I was nothing and had no impact on his life. Making it out that I rejected him in the hotel room and that that was it rather than actually listening to me in that moment when I'd explained it was coming, but turned out he knew it never was.

He said, "I was closed off and never opened up to him."

Was he right?

I got that message and blacked out. I know I messaged him back some fucked up essay but honestly, I cannot remember what I said and thank god for having the iMessage 'erase all messages after one year' function switched on to preserve stupid cloud storage because frankly, I don't want to go back and see what I wrote.

We didn't speak again. It was rough. I was so upset however over the course of the following months I came to realise there were things he was completely right about.

I wasn't opening up to him as much as I thought I'd been doing. I was supportive and caring, but I don't think he knew even half as much about me as I knew about him. I didn't give out much about me and my past as I'd thought.

I also analysed it all and realised, whilst I did want to be in a relationship with him, I wasn't proud of him.

None of my friends had met him. Aileen included and we lived together. My parents didn't even know I was seeing someone. No one knew. A couple people from work knew I was seeing someone but no one was excited about it. They later told me they weren't excited about it because I didn't express any excitement about it. It was as if it was just someone I was seeing for a while but I was never serious.

I didn't know how to dissect this any further. I was just numb to the idea of Andrew.

I was upset.

Damien

I was done being upset after a couple of months. Done sitting around being sad. I was ready to re-join the world. I was ready to be a slut.

I downloaded the apps, deleted Andrew's existence from them so I couldn't be sad about it any more, and started being the slut I needed to be. You know, that's the right way to get over a guy isn't it?

I met up with a bunch of guys. Had my fun. Had THEIR fun. It was fun for everyone.

A buffet of men who it was almost like they'd been waiting for me to re-join the apps again.

Lots of 'Welcome back's'. I felt almost famous.

The sadness would kick in every now and then and I'd think, *Omg they're all still here*, like they'd never even aimed on leaving the apps. Just little digital men trying to find their next digital dick and the one after that. I was their next digital dick.

Then the confidence would kick in again and I'd go, *And they're my next digital dick.*

I knew it was unhealthy in long form, however, for the time being, it was exactly what my mind needed to process... or not process... everything I'd just gone through and from then on tried to avoid.

I was being a slut.

All my friends were proud, I was getting out there again. I had stories to tell at the work coffee machine. I had stories again! Not ones that were sad and embarrassing, but ones that made everyone go, "Fuck yes, Morgan go you!" again.

God, I'd missed those.

BUT I DIDN'T MISS ANDREW NOPE NAH NOOOO – that thought kept going through my head.

But then came Damien again.

Damien messaged me and he wasn't seeing anyone.

And I wasn't seeing anyone...

And the sex was mind-blowingly amazing, just as I remembered it.

So over the course of the next couple of weeks, we kept talking... and yeah, that was back on.

It was kind of perfect having someone a second away from

his phone ready to come over whenever I wanted it.

I felt powerful. In a fucked up way, but also in a way that made me still feel wanted.

We would meet at mine (never his) and do whatever it was (you know what it was) once a week.

This later turned into two times a week... and eventually, three times a week.

This went on for months. It was perfect for me.

No attachment, no labels, regular sex. What else did I need? Oh, wait... I did want a relationship still... but Damien's good for now.

Damien and I had an unspoken agreement that it was just what it was. And I loved that.

I knew I couldn't do anything more than what it was because at the end of the day, I really cared about him still. Sure, we would go at it like wild rabbits, but we would always end up talking for hours and hours and venting to each other.

I realised, I actually knew him more than I ever knew Andrew. And Damien knew me more than Andrew ever did, yet I'd never even seen this man outside of my house. It was so obscure to me to think he knew so much about me yet this was the reality.

Damien and I kept this thing going for ages. I always knew he wanted more from me but I couldn't handle that. It's not that I didn't want it from anyone, I really did want it, but it's also that I knew I didn't want THAT from him. I cared for him more than anyone else. He didn't have the best mental health, neither did I. We checked in on each other all the time. But I didn't feel anything romantic for the man like he did for me. We never really brought it up, we just kept doing what we were doing.

I guess because I was the one on the other side of it I felt like it was OK. But I also knew I couldn't continue doing this to someone forever. At one point I'd have to walk away so he could go and be free and find what he wanted with me with someone else, but the selfish part of me wanted to keep hold of it until I found that next one myself. And... that's what ended up happening.

K

I was on the apps again, being my slutty self.

Someone popped up giving me a little tap. I thought he was really cute. Not my usual type. Kind of looked like Damien but I was more attracted to this one and intrigued. Still short (ok slightly taller than me… slightly), still stumpy but this time muscular, and I could see this guy took some pride in his appearance. Clean shaven, tidy haircut. Fresh.

I tapped him back. I felt like a little school girl and THAT'S how I knew it was something immediately exciting.

He was a couple of kilometres away from me. Achievable. Easy. Great.

We both looked at each other's profiles but neither of us spoke, so I left it at that.

A couple days later, I got a new match on another dating app.

It was the same guy. I must have swiped right on him when I didn't even recognise him on the other app. They were different pictures after all. Whatever. I finally had this match though so I had his name (as opposed to just a 'K' on the first app). I tried to read it, but I couldn't even pronounce it. That was hot.

I bit the bullet and messaged him. He messaged back pretty quickly. The conversation started and I was immediately hooked. I hadn't felt like this with someone in a long time. I hadn't had butterflies for an even longer time. It was all so cute, just cute.

We spoke from then on literally nonstop. He told me he was getting in trouble at work because he kept going on his phone to talk to me. I didn't even know what he did for work. My work didn't care, so he must have had the kind of job where he couldn't be on his phone, but I thought it was adorable that he continued to do it knowing he'd get into trouble. Like he didn't care about work, he just wanted to talk to me.

We were obsessed with each other. We'd talk all day every day.

But soon I noticed, when we matched on one app and tapped each other on the other, he was 2kms from me. Little did I know until later he lived 20kms from me. He just happened to be in the area at that time. But the spark was there. I didn't care.

After a bit over a month of nonstop talking, it had gotten to the point where he wanted to finally meet up. I was so obsessed with the spark of it all being digital and text message that I wasn't sure if I was ready to actually face him.

We knew it would just be sex. We both talked about it. He said that's all he wanted and if something happened in the future then something happened in the future. That was something that was very much up my alley. I went through life with a similar mind-set. I was open to whatever came. But was I ready to actually face him?

Another couple of weeks had gone by. He'd brought up again that he wanted to see me. He really wanted to see me. I kept deferring the conversation. I don't know why. I think I liked what it was so much I didn't want to not feel the spark or butterflies when it was standing right in front of me. I was hooked on what it was. I didn't want that to go away, or change, or die. I didn't want to risk it.

We both had the day off of work, so I finally gave in and told him my address. He immediately sent me a live pin of his location and said, *I'm on my way*. I could see on his location he wasn't even close by. It was going to take him at LEAST an hour and a half to turn up.

The anxiety kicked in. Do I cancel? Do I just wait it out? Do I just sit here freaking out in my head that he's a serial killer and going to come over to my house and murder me?

Then it crossed my mind... I'd never even heard him speak. I knew his name... but I didn't even know how to pronounce it. WHAT DO I SAY?

As his location was getting closer, my anxiety was getting higher. I didn't know what to do. He'd messaged me saying he was so excited to finally meet me but I was scared it was going to be purely transactional.

He was ten minutes away.

I got a text from Damien at that moment asking if I was free. I ignored it.

K texted me, *I'm here.*

Followed by a little knock at the door.

I opened the door, we looked into each other's eyes, he smiled, and I launched and kissed him. He was adorable. He was exactly like I'd imagined. I didn't even speak, we just made out and I dragged him to my bed. It was hot. It all just took over me and I was so happy to finally have this moment with him.

An hour or so went by. I repeat, it was hot. We finished and lay in bed talking for a bit.

He said, "You know we just did all of that and I'm only hearing you speak now," and we laughed. That's something I vividly remember about him. We laughed a lot. It was sort of electric. Something I hadn't had with someone so strong from the get go. We kept talking for a while then he eventually left. When he was leaving he didn't want to let me go or stop kissing me, but he had to get home and I had to mentally freak out on my own.

We kept talking the second he left.

I haven't even properly named him yet in this story. What would his name be? Something with a K but not something that will give his true identity away. There are no good K names that would suit him. Wow, there really isn't. I can't just call him K, can I? Actually, come to think of it, 'K' might be the perfect name for the fucker.

On reflection, 'K' is extremely fitting for him. He doesn't deserve a name. He deserves something short and blunt, just K.

A note to all of you reading, whilst everyone in this story has done a number on me, K is really the one that fucked me up the most. By all means, hate on him as much as you like. Burn in hell.

OK, back to the story Morgan. Fuck, sorry I got a little carried away.

He left and my brain was swooning. I hadn't felt butterflies like this for a long time. Not since Andrew really. Not with anyone.

I don't know what it was but I could hear my brain saying what it tended to always say, *Just go with it.*

Did I like him? Was I just falling for a mildly attractive man with an accent? That's right. An ACCENT. I didn't even know what accent it was because I didn't ask where he was from. I just found it fucking hot.

We agreed to hang out again… and again… and eventually, we were hanging out whenever we could. We weren't seeing each other that much because he lived so far away and we didn't even have the same days off during the week. He had Tuesdays and Wednesdays off, I had weekends. It was actually really difficult to manage. He also lived with family, not his parents or anything, but a married cousin and her husband and baby, so I was fine when he said he didn't want to bring me into that environment.

Before you read the above and think, oh god, no, he's married, this is a lie, this actually is the complete truth. He's not married, the baby isn't his. Although, when I first heard it, like you might have, the thought definitely went through my mind.

He was always very honest with me, however stubborn. He told me he wasn't looking for a relationship, but he liked me and he wanted to see where it would go. When we started, whatever it was, I wasn't looking for a relationship either. I was still focussed on saving money for my future home, future travels, very career focussed and trying to move up the ladder in life. I couldn't handle a boyfriend on top of that. Little did I know the way I was acting with him, I was giving the boyfriend work but not getting the boyfriend's effort.

I felt our feelings for each other growing, which was great, but in my mind I thought it was growing for both of us. I don't think in hindsight it was for him.

We saw each other like I said, as much as we could. It wasn't that frequent, sometimes once a week, then once a fortnight, then once a month, but spoke still all day everyday. I was hooked. Whatever he was selling me, I was buying it.

But I knew it would get to the point where one of us would

have to budge. And I knew it was going to be me.

He was getting exactly what he wanted from me, but I was starting to want more. I understood where he'd told me he didn't want a relationship, but he also put into my mind that if it happened in the future it happened in the future. That to me sounded like he was at least open to the idea of something organically developing, which was enough for me to go off.

Me, being the little bitch I am, started playing mind games. Not messaging him back immediately. Leaving him on read. Trying to get as much effort as I could out of him. Not replying to his messages, just liking the comment every so often. Seeing what I could get out of this man with minimal effort.

I mean, in my defence, at this point it's been about four months and neither of us were openly coming to the table ready for a discussion. So yeah, I let the toxicity take over my brain as I didn't want to be the one to bring up the whole conversation. I was fucking terrified. I didn't want to bring it up and it completely blow up in my face. I really didn't want it to end. So fuck it, I got toxic.

Turns out he wasn't getting it. He thought I was just showing I wasn't interested. We spoke properly about it and I ended up apologising for playing games. It was childish. He said it was OK and he was sorry I felt the need to do it. I expressed to him I didn't want to keep seeing him if there wasn't a chance at there being a relationship. I was ready for something more. Something substantial.

He thought about it overnight, and told me he couldn't give me something he didn't feel he was ready for and that he wished to keep doing what we were doing until maybe the day he was ready came along. I didn't like the uncertainty. It made me feel really used. Here I was again, giving the boyfriend experience without being someone's actual fucking boyfriend. I had to remember that in that scenario he was literally getting exactly what he wanted out of it but I wasn't. I literally expressed to him what I wanted and got denied, but I couldn't just give in and continue not getting what I wanted out of it. I knew it would just make things worse and make me even more upset in the future.

I ended it. It killed me. This was someone I really truly liked and wanted to proudly call my boyfriend, but he didn't want to call me that. I felt rejected, like I was made to believe it was leading somewhere when it wasn't. I tried not to speak to him for months, we didn't. He tried talking to me. I ignored it, or if I couldn't ignore it, I was snappy.

How could I let someone come into my life claiming they were open to a relationship if it ended up just happening? Oh wait, he literally said, he didn't want a relationship. He then also said that if one just ended up happening then he was open to it. Or did he? Was I imagining this? Did we even have that conversation or did I just completely make it up because it's what I wanted to hear? Fuck, this is what he's done to me. Actually made me doubt what I knew I'd heard! He was the one who'd said he was open to it if it came his way. Turns out he wasn't open at all, or at least not with me anyway... but he still couldn't just say that.

He'd made me feel like I wasn't good enough, like I wasn't worth it. Luckily for me this is unfortunately something I'm used to feeling. Feeling like I'm not worth the fight. Not worth the struggle. Not worth the time. I once again felt completely thrown away like I'm not worthy. I hated when people made me feel like this because deep down I know I'm fucking worth the time and energy.

I'd never felt so pathetic. Overthinking every single thought and feeling I'd ever had for this person. Trying to find the part I'd missed. Trying to dissect everything we'd gone through together to actually decipher where it all went wrong in my mind. All of this overthinking was exhausting, but what I knew I could do successfully without too much overthinking, was hate him.

This all went down at the end of 2019. Before the world started to crumble and burn in flames (not just figuratively, but literally since I live in Australia and the country not long after caught on fire).

2020 Hit

2020 hit. And so did the reality of stepping on a set of scales. I weighed myself for the first time in years. I already wasn't happy with my body, but I never really was. But after seeing that number on the scales staring back at me, I REALLY wasn't. I was shocked. This was way higher than the number I mentally thought I was. I immediately knew I had to do something about it. I bought an at-home treadmill that night and started thinking about diets and exercise.

Although it was bad news, it also was good. I had something to focus my time and energy on that was motivating and healthy. Bear in mind, I think my age at this point is twenty-seven. I know I keep jumping from ages, but really that's just how time flies (sucks).

All I could think about was how K was going to miss out on me and my new body. I was hitting the diet and exercising hard. Really hard. And it was working! We didn't speak but I could see that he'd see what I was doing on social media. He was reacting to it and saying he was happy for me at times, but I wasn't giving him the attention. All I could focus on was my Khloe Kardashian Revenge Body and how I would shove it in his face and look hot.

After about two months, I'd lost a substantial amount of

weight and it was noticeable. People at work were all commenting on it. Friends were all super impressed. When anyone asked about what I was doing everyone was realising I was doing everything really healthily even though within a short amount of time it shouldn't have been as healthy as it was.

But by this time, it's March... the pandemic is coming in hard. I was the last person at work to be sent home with a work from home laptop. Literally, sitting in the office by myself everyday waiting to be handed a device that would let me do what everyone in the company was doing. I was wasting my time making stupid videos at the office, of which everyone from work would see and laugh and I loved it.

Everyone loved it including K. Still reacting to everything I was doing on social media, he kept trying to get my attention like I was getting his. I finally got the work laptop and was sent home from the office to work from then on.

The company I was working for was going through a corporate sale. The business was being sold to another company, and for a few months I'd known I didn't have a job at the new business and was being made redundant. With the pandemic coming in hard and heavy, this was kind of good news considering I was reading all over the news that people were losing their jobs out of nowhere due to the pandemic. At least I knew no matter what I was having a huge chunk of money thrown into my lap, so it was a little sense of security.

By April, I'm working from home, smashing my laptop, barely any work to do considering all of my clients had tapped out of our business knowing the money was just going to another company. I literally had nothing to do at work but sit there. My boss would call me simply to check I was alive. I'd go on huge walks to exercise with my phone and just talk to everyone I worked with whilst exercising. It was kind of great.

Then, May 1 came quickly. My first day of no work. No job. No income.

I went in and dropped off my laptop. Timed it right with a friend from work who I hadn't seen in months. We all had to go in at 15 minute intervals so we didn't connect because of the pandemic, but she and I timed it as we didn't care. We hung out for a little bit after, had a cigarette outside and finally said our goodbyes. We said we'd keep in contact. I think we both knew that we probably wouldn't. And that was right, we didn't. But it was still a beautiful moment to have with someone I cared for.

So I'm sitting there, barbecue sauce on my titties (I'm kidding).

So I'm sitting there, first week, isolated at home, half the country has just been burnt down due to the fires (yay Australia). I have no job. I'm not allowed to hang out with friends. My money is just going to burn down like the country did and we didn't see an end in sight whatsoever.

This was actually a time I can refer to as 'The Pandoodle'. I know the word 'pandemic' is pretty triggering to all of us by this stage, but really, pandoodle kind of describes it better. I like calling it that because I was living in my own little world, literally alone. Sat there, twiddling my thumbs, watching the same YouTube vlogs on repeat instead of watching ANYTHING on the various TV streaming lists that we were all giving each other. Going from all of that to doom scrolling on social media, laughing and smiling at the wall, doing a stand-up comedy routine to the dead flowers on my dining table that I'd picked on my daily hot-girl exercise walk in attempt to make myself smile. That smile was short-lived.

Pandoodle perfectly describes it. It was a time where we all literally let the crazy old lady that lives inside of our heads go from worrying, then to laughing, then to singing *lalalaaaaa* whilst rocking back and forth. I'd often forget to simply speak and next thing it'd been days, since I'd said a word. When you finally opened your mouth and said 'hello' it sounded like you'd just come out of a coma. One of the main things that kept me grounded though were the daily cigarettes on the front steps of my apartment block with my neighbour, of whom now I have absolutely no recollection of their name.

Oh well. Pandoodle black out.

We'd just sit there to keep each other company until all of a sudden, they'd say something like

"It's gonna rain later."

Which would get me to respond with;

"Yeah. Looks like it."

Absolutely gripping conversation. I'd put my cigarette out and go

"Same time tomorrow?"

"Yep, see you here!"

And I'd run back inside.

About a week goes by, I still have my dieting and exercise keeping me motivated. Oh, and my daily cigarette with my unnamed neighbour. I hold onto it like it's the one thing I've got, because really, it was the one thing I had keeping me motivated and going.

I finally got a message from K. Not a social media reaction to something I'd posted, a real message finally checking in as he could literally watch every day that I was either in the process of losing my career and sitting around bored or out walking all on my own. We ended up speaking for a bit.

How've you been? I wanted to check in as I know you've just lost your job.

Hey! Yeah I'm OK. I knew it was coming for ages so I was as ready as I could have been. It's just super weird.

I can only imagine. Are you really OK?

Yeah, why?

You're just losing a lot of weight.

Yeah, because I want to.

It's not because of me is it?

No?

It's just it all started just after we stopped seeing each other and I was worried. I liked you how you were I didn't think you needed to change.

I did all of this for myself. I wasn't happy with how I looked and I didn't realise I'd gotten as big as I had.

You didn't realise!?!?!?

... yeah.

You didn't realise? Really? Ha!

Excuse me.

I'm just kidding, you're beautiful.

Thanks... but did you just laugh at me, call me fat and then try to make it OK by calling me beautiful.

It was a joke.

Well, maybe if we were on better terms it would have been taken better but maybe don't refer to someone as fat.

I didn't call you fat.

You kind of did. Anyway, have a good week!

That's it?

What do you want me to say?

OK fine.

Why would anyone make fun of something else's body like that? I was receiving messages from other people congratulating me and telling me I was amazing. You know, SHOWING ACTUAL SUPPORT. Yet the person I thought I was closest to was making fun of it and essentially fat shaming me? Joke or not, that's so fucked up to poke at someone's obvious insecurity. Sure, I'd never said the words 'I'm insecure about my body' but isn't it safe to assume if someone's losing a lot of weight, they most likely are insecure about their body? And sorry, joke or not, it's not OK to EVER talk about someone's body like that.

This exchange motivated me even more. I wanted to work out even harder and post about it on social media and for him to see it and it essentially to be like a huge FUCK YOU in his face.

He watched everything. I felt empowered. Fucking bastard called me fat (I know he didn't literally but come on, he fucking did).

Towards the end of May, Aileen, turned to me and told me she was moving out. Nothing to do with us, she'd been with her boyfriend for a really long time and they'd finally decided it was time to give living together a go. I was happy for them, but really, it caused a lot of stress for me as I'd just finished my job with no prospects of another one coming anytime soon, the pandemic was a giant beast and the rental market was terrifying. I luckily could afford to live by myself, so I ended up staying in the apartment and living alone for a while. I thought it'd be good for me. Another fucking fresh start.

K

June rolled around, I had made the conscious effort to only step on the scales every two weeks or once a month so I didn't become obsessive. June 7, I hit my target. 10kgs had fallen off of me. I had never felt better but I knew I wasn't done. My target was to get fine with my routine and body so that I could ease off the diet and maintain the weight I was on.

I started to do that. Life was getting happier. I was finally a bit more confident.

I posted about hitting my 10kg target on social media. K saw it pretty quickly.

He messaged me and said congratulations.

That played on my mind. The pandemic was so lonely and miserable that I mistook him saying one fucking word for him caring. I thought it was the sweetest thing because, well, it was sweet. All my friends had said to me something along the lines of 'fuck yeah' but he took the time out of his day to say one word less than them... but it was a really long word. So much effort, so caring and thoughtful. Fuck why is my brain like this?

Next thing... I'm messaging him back... SHIT!

The conversation went pretty quickly into how we used to see each other and he said he wanted to see me again. I was getting the butterflies again. He was getting what he wanted, and so was I in that moment. I was getting butterflies. That's what I wanted. Sure, Morgan, fucking lie to yourself.

I thought, this is it, he's finally ready.

We made a plan to see each other a week later. It was like time hadn't passed. We didn't kiss, we met up and got the train into the city together and walked around talking nonstop. We literally didn't stop talking the entire time, the chemistry was just how I had remembered it. It was like those few months apart had recharged it and when we finally reconnected it was full blast.

He eventually tried to hold my hand, something he'd never done before even when we were seeing each other the first time. I resisted and brushed it off but he kept trying.

After about four attempts, he stopped and looked at me and went, "Can you just hold my fucking hand?"

I gave in. He wanted it. I wanted it but I couldn't continue resisting what I knew we both wanted.

I held his hand. We both smiled and kept walking. He held my hand for roughly 3kms of walking through the city. It was cute. Butterflies going through my whole body. I was scared I couldn't control it any more and I'd completely given in.

We'd spent hours and hours together wandering around. We eventually went and ate dinner somewhere. I cannot for the life of me remember where but also keep in mind, COVID's happening, a lot of restaurants were shut so I remember it not being easy to even find a good place open.

We knew we both needed to go home after dinner. When saying goodbye there was a hug which lasted a really long time. I was into it, but I couldn't kiss him yet. I didn't want to fully give in too quickly. I needed this time for it to be real, not just about sex.

I headed home and before I even made it home, he'd messaged me.

Thank you for today. I'd really missed you.

I remember screenshotting it and wanting to send it to my friends to be like WE'RE BACK but reality kicked in and I realised I hadn't even spoken to any of my friends yet about how I was revisiting it. Was that bad? Was I keeping it a secret on purpose? This played on my mind for a while longer.

I hadn't told anyone.

I didn't want to. I knew my brain was overthinking every single detail of us hanging out and speaking again. I knew I was getting ahead of reality. I could feel the butterflies taking over my brain and mistaking someone simply holding my hand for them saying they wanted to be with me. I kept trying to tell myself that it was just someone holding my hand and a flirty moment, but my brain just kept playing things over and over telling me it was more than what it was.

Fuck. All those strong feelings of liking this guy had all come back. I couldn't suppress it any more.

I knew I had to finally tell my friend Noni that I was giving him another chance. She wasn't that impressed but when I explained how he was behaving differently. She was a little bit excited because she believed he'd changed.

Noni was someone I could turn to for a lot of venting and emotional support. We kind of did that for each other. She would vent to me a million different issues and I would rationalise all of them for her, helping her actually see the situation clearly. I was good at rationalising other people's thoughts, but never my own. She was the best at helping me rationalise my own, never quite to the level I needed them to be rationalised to, but close. Close enough for me to be able to finish rationalising it all myself. But keep in mind, I feel like I'm a psycho in my brain, so really she was doing God's work.

She was on board. But, she was the only person for months that knew.

K and I would continue seeing each other, this time it was a lot more romantic, or at least I saw it that way. In hindsight, it wasn't romantic at all, my brain was just playing tricks on me to believe it was.

Whenever we were together we couldn't keep our hands off

each other. I wasn't working because of the pandemic, he still was, but this allowed Tuesdays and Wednesdays to be our days. We were seeing each other more frequently, but it was still playing on my mind where it was going.

When we first discussed reconnecting, he said that he was always open to life bringing him a relationship, but he just knew he wasn't ready. I remember thinking that was OK because I was truly someone who believed in never knowing if one was really ready. I never sought out a relationship. I always tried to be at least a little bit open minded if something developed into a relationship, but I wasn't solely hunting one down. It was more about the connection with someone for me than it was about finding a relationship.

I vividly remember one day. I was completely blinded by my feelings for this man over the reality of how he'd treated me. He'd stayed the night at his best friend's house which wasn't that far from where I lived at the time. She randomly had a business meeting the next day in the suburb that I lived so he called me to see if I wanted to get lunch with them. I was a little nervous. He'd spoken about her many times before. This was his BEST friend, so that immediately put pressure in my mind to perform, but also not perform because I need to be myself. Shit. Here we go with the overthinking.

He called me in the morning and said, "We're on our way now, we'll be 30 minutes."

"OK, easy. Where will I meet you?"

"I'll send you the address of where we're going and meet us there."

"Sweet."

K sent me the address. It was only about four blocks from me, so I knew I had plenty of time.

30 minutes rolled by and I walked over. As I turned the corner onto the street, he was already waiting outside the front of the house for me to arrive. We saw each other, both with huge smiles, and he started running up to me. He got to me and grabbed my face and kissed me and lifted me. What the hell? He seemed so excited to see me!

He put me down, held my hand, we walked back closer to the address and waited for his friend to wrap up the meeting. He said it'd only be about 10 more minutes.

During those 10 minutes, he just kept grabbing my face and kissing me. Didn't stop. It was crazy to me. He was acting like someone in high school with the biggest crush. This was one of the rare times he'd show any form of affection. Something I'd always craved but never really got from him. Like I said, rare.

I remember he lifted me and popped me to sit on this raised concrete slab. Our eyes were level but he liked that so I could wrap around him like a koala. As he's kissing me, his hands go to my waist, and I feel him grab my love handles. He pulled back, smiled, looked me in the eyes and said, "Still a little bit of weight to lose."

I was gob smacked.

"What?"

"No no. Don't get angry. I was just kidding."

At that exact second his best friend came out to find us. Saved by the FUCKING bell, K.

"Is that the famous Morgan?"

"Hi!"

"Honestly, it's so lovely to finally meet the man this one won't stop raving about."

"OH REEEEEALLY?"

I looked at K and smiled. Even after literally insulting me, hearing that he's been raving about me to his friends overruled that. Fucking idiot Morgan how DESPERATE are you.

K started blushing and quickly ushered us all to get in his friend's car.

As we're driving, only for about 5 minutes to the cafe, K's friend goes, "I must say Morgan you look very different to the picture's I've seen of you."

"Oh really?"

"Yeah, you look great!"

"Well, I guess that all depends on the pictures you've seen of me."

K quickly interjects here to go;

"Oh, I've only shown her photos from when you were fat."

"K," said his best friend.

The car went silent for a very uncomfortable 15 seconds.

"I didn't mean it like that. They're just my favourite photos of you," K said.

"Yep, sure."

His best friend smacked him on the arm whilst she was driving

"Thank you!" I said.

"Absolutely, he deserved that." We laughed.

She then parked the car, and we hopped out. Walked into the cafe, quickly ordered food and coffee. Damn, I needed a strong coffee.

K sat next to me with his hand on my thigh. I'm talking non-stop to his best friend. After she'd smacked him across the arm, I knew this is someone I'm going to like.

The conversation flowed easily. The coffees and food came. Chit chat was organic and seamless. Even when eating, K's hand left my thigh only to quickly cut up all his food into bite sized pieces so that he could reattach it to my thigh once again and eat one handed. I watched him do that and we both smiled, and he leant in and kissed me. Back to eating now. I was starving.

As we're wrapping up lunch his best friend brought up a rather, specific conversation;

"So, if you don't mind me asking."

"No, go for it," I said, not realising where the conversation was REALLY going to go.

"How long have you been clean for now?"

"Clean?"

"Yeah. From the drugs?"

"What?"

K looked at me with this confused face whilst I looked at him with a confused face. I grabbed his hand from my thigh and removed it.

K followed up and said;

"You told me you'd done hard drugs."

"No, I hadn't."

"Yes, you had."

"No… I hadn't. And I wouldn't have because I have never done hard drugs."

I'd told him I'd been a bit of a party boy years prior and done clubbing drugs, but not hard drugs because I'D NEVER DONE HARD DRUGS!

The look of absolute distaste that his best friend was giving him at this point was laughable. She went;

"K, you told all of us he was an ex-drug addict!"

"Told you ALL what?"

"Well, that's what I thought you told me." K went.

"No no no, we're not putting words in my mouth. That's a HUGE thing to mistake me saying and you've what, gone and told all your friends I'm a drug addict?"

"Not all of my friends."

"K," his best friend said, stern and direct, almost like telling him to stop talking.

His best friend continued talking to me;

"I'm sorry Morgan. I shouldn't have brought it up. I guess it was all a huge misunderstanding."

"No, it's OK, it's not your fault," I said directly to his best friend. "You weren't to know. If I'm honest, I did have a pretty big phase in my late teens and early twenties of partying a lot, especially when I was living in London and using clubbing drugs a little too frequently. But by no means am I a drug addict or addicted to anything besides, well, cigarettes. But if you could please go around and tell his friends the truth that would be excellent!"

"Will do," she said, and we had a laugh. She got up and went to use the bathroom.

K sat in silence looking at me and tapping my thigh again with his fingers. You could see his brain trying to think of what to say to me whilst it was just the two of us for a short minute.

"I got it wrong, but at the same time you just have that look."

"What look?"

"You just kind of look a little bit druggy."

I looked him in the eye, smiled and just said, "Stop."

I then giggled because by this point, I really wanted the conversation to be over. I brushed it off the best way I knew how to. Laugh and move the conversation along.

The best friend came back to the table and went "OK, let's go."

"Sweet, let's go pay," said K.

"No, no, that's already done."

"Wait, what?" I went.

"I've paid. It's the least I could do for him embarrassing the heck out of you."

We all laughed. We walked on and got in the car, and she drove me back to my apartment.

"Can I come to yours now?" said K.

"Sure, if you want."

We got out of the car after she'd driven to my apartment. I hopped out and did the whole 'It was so lovely to finally meet you' sign off. I liked her. She was nice and I could see she really cared about him.

We went inside and sat on the couch. I was in a little bit of a food coma but also quite tired from being on my best behaviour, so I popped on the TV. K lay on the couch and said to lean on him. Kind of like spooning but not. He's back to being the affectionate K I rarely got but for today, I was taking full advantage of. He was playing with my hair.

"You do know your hair is falling out."

"What?" I looked at him.

"Yeah, it's thinning and your hairline's going back."

"Well, I'm not surprised. I know my genetics, plus I've gone blonde myself so many times I'm sure the bleach has had some affect."

"No, you're going bald."

Ok, by this point, I'm getting sick of it.

"Ok, no, I'm not, that's being a bit dramatic."

"You are I can see it!"

"K, can you just stop?"

Silence.

I wasn't insecure about my hair or hairline before… but now I fucking was. Why was he poking at me all day long? If his excuse was that he was joking, then he'd taken it all too fucking far. But also, none of these were jokes. Grabbing my love handles and telling me I had more weight to lose? Telling his friends I was a recovering drug addict? And now telling me I'm losing my hair? Wow I've really hit the jackpot with this man haven't I!

K got up to use the bathroom and when he came back, he went;

"OK, can we have sex now?"

I sat there with a kind of puzzled and shocked expression on my face.

"Is that why you wanted to come over?"

"I mean, not entirely, but I want to have sex."

"Well, I'm not really feeling it right now."

"OK, fine."

It suddenly got a bit awkward. He sat back on the couch and resumed positions. This time not playing with my hair at all and he was on his phone. I tried not to read into it until 5 minutes later when he said;

"OK, I'm going to go. Work's messaged me saying they need me to come in."

K very abruptly packed everything up and left my apartment. I sat on the couch kind of in shock. Did he literally just want to hang out with me to have sex? All these horrible thoughts were going through my mind. I kept going from one side where he'd been acting really romantic (or so my delusional brain was thinking he was) to remembering he'd poked fun at my weight, my hairline, told all his friends I was a drug addict and now I sat there feeling like the man didn't want a bar of me if I wasn't going to give him sex. What the fuck?

I didn't message him the whole afternoon. And I didn't hear from him until maybe 7p.m. that evening when he messaged me saying he wished he'd stayed at mine and not gone to work. I messaged back a little bit short because I was still kind of confused, but I didn't want to talk about it. I also knew I didn't want to feel like that again, but me being lonely, I brushed it to the side.

Part of me wondered for a while if he'd literally left mine abruptly to go have sex with someone else. I didn't fully trust that his work needed him. This man had made me into the most insecure version of myself. He'd made fun of my appearance in different ways, my lifestyle and made-up stories about me, and now I was growing to not fully trust him. I felt backed into a corner because I couldn't be angry at him as we weren't in a relationship technically, but I also knew I didn't want to feel like this.

A couple more months rolled by, I was starting to feel lonelier than ever before. By this stage I was still living by myself, not working, dealing with the depression of the pandemic, but getting the support I needed from someone only once or twice a week. I craved more. I wanted to go back to work and I wanted to see K a lot more than I was.

I think something I haven't mentioned during the whole spiel is that he never stayed over and I would never stay at his place. He liked 'sleeping in his own bed' and that was his reasoning. I was so lonely I saw that as being OK. He stayed over once. Only ever once. I thought it was normal, but bear in mind, I've never had a normal relationship with anyone. Red flag!

The couple of months that rolled by I was finally starting to feel a bit of reality tell me that this entire situation was fucking bullshit. He wanted to see me again. He was acting more romantic and more connected than we were the first time, but it wasn't going anywhere. I got one opportunity to have him stay over and that was it. This is someone I'd known by this point for nine months, and sure, we weren't seeing each other for maybe two or three in the middle, but add it together that's still six to seven months of 'seeing' someone. Not even 'dating'. I don't even know if I know the actual fucking difference, or if there, even, is a difference. Is there? Or has modern dating become so manipulating that we've convinced each other there's a difference between 'seeing' and 'dating' someone. Literally, what is the difference? I bet we all have our own VERY different definitions.

Regardless, I was growing impatient. Enough was enough. I couldn't bear it any more feeling like someone's side hustle.

I brought it up.

Word vomit was coming out of my mouth.

I just kept spewing.

The longest fucking essay text message, because despite being twenty-seven, I acted like a fucking child when I didn't get what I wanted and felt neglected. But fuck being told I was being immature, you're literally leading me on and getting what you want but again, I'm not getting what I want from this stupid situation.

Annoyingly, I didn't say any of it like this.

It was 'heartfelt' – I wanted it to show that I cared about him as deeply as I did and I saw a future and wanted it to be something really amazing because I knew if given the opportunity, it would have been. Did I know what that future exactly looked like? No. Did I realise later in life that that kind of sentence scared the shit out of men? Yes. Did I actually care? No! I never saw it as being something scary, it just simply meant to me that yes I see a future, I don't know what that looks like but it's more that I see you in my future because I don't see this ending. Not scary, actually fucking romantic and real.

He opened the message. Then he said, *I understand, but I'm not ready*, and that was that.

Like a fucking bullet to the chest. That. Was. That.

Another reason why his name is just 'K'. He was short and direct with me. I never got clarity or any real answers. Just bluntness.

It was done. Not only was I living alone during a pandemic, but I was completely and utterly alone in my relationship. Wait, I was always single. I've literally been technically single, since I was seventeen. GREAT. Here we are again. Back to the fucking beginning.

K

After that I remember, I didn't speak to him for about a week or so. I didn't want to speak to him and act like what I'd said was just brushed under the carpet. It meant a lot to me to make sure I'd been heard and addressed properly. But in the pandemic, a week felt like a month.

Both K and I had become quite mentally dependent on each other because of the pandemic. We supported each other, entertained each other, and kept each other company even when apart. Living alone during a pandemic wasn't a smart choice in hindsight, but frankly I don't think I could have gone through a lot of what was happening with someone else on the couch next to me, everyday complaining about it as well.

Sometimes it was nice to be completely alone during the craziness of the real world happening outside. It was like existing in my own little world where outside of the walls of my apartment something else was happening, but I was safe inside. Literally, that's exactly what it was, not safe outside, but my own little world in my apartment, that was mine. My little pandoodle.

K and I obviously didn't talk as much as we used to, but we still spoke a bit. I took the weeks I needed to really try to move on from what had happened. I tried my best to ignore it. I didn't want to fall back into it because I knew it was going to become toxic. It's unbalanced if only one person is getting what they want out of a connection but at the same time, I was addicted to it.

He knew he couldn't talk to me in the same manner that we once spoke. Seeing each other in the flesh wasn't an option any longer and I'd put my foot down about that. As the pandemic got more and more fucked up, video calling became normal for everyone, and it became normal for K and I as well.

We ended up speaking over the phone on video almost every single day for weeks. He would ask what I did that day, "I did my walk and sat on the couch and watched TV all day… again… this is my life now."

"Yeah, I went to work and wore a mask all day and now my skin is breaking out in acne."

That was it, everyday. But there came a comfort with just knowing we had each other to talk to especially in a time where we really didn't feel like we had anyone.

It became so routine that I knew he'd call every night. Like clockwork, he'd call around 8p.m. after he'd finished work and gone to the gym.

It was a weird comfort in knowing it wasn't just friendship, but best friendship, and really just burying how we felt about each other in order to keep that connection. I knew what we were doing was silly, and would probably hurt the fucking shit out of me in the long run, but I couldn't stop, and I think he knew all of that too. We just were obsessed with each other. I knew this because his friends would ask about me all the time. They'd ask him how I was going, so I knew he was speaking about me to them and letting them know he cared about me.

Only Noni really knew the ins and outs about him and I on my side of things. I'd not told anyone. Because it'd never gotten to a point in whatever we were doing that I felt the need to announce to the world that I had a man or someone or even just a boy? I didn't even know what to call K but the idea of actually referring to him as nothing but a 'friend' physically made me feel sick.

Some good news finally ended up coming my way. I got a job. It wasn't one that I was necessarily excited for, but by this point it was October and I hadn't worked for five months, so I was just READY to deep dive into doing something that motivated me again besides losing weight.

I remember getting off the call from my soon-to-be boss and immediately telling K. He was thrilled. He was so happy that I got a job and I was feeling like I was finally getting back on top of my career because he knew how important having a career was for me. He kept messaging me saying congratulations every day for a week. For some reason I took it as a huge sign that he was supportive about this. Because he was! It made me really happy.

He wanted to take me out for dinner and a drink to celebrate the weekend before I started working. I agreed and said, "Look I can't really afford much because I haven't been working but I'm totally down for this and excited to see where you take me."

He took me to the Hard Rock Cafe…

I wouldn't necessarily call that romantic, but then again, we were just friends I guess.

It was still confusing, a man I liked but wasn't allowed to like, taking me out to dinner to celebrate my career. But it's not a date, but it's totally a date, but it's still not a date?

The dinner was fine, not the best food. Just a fucking burger, but I was just so swooned by this man that it didn't fucking matter. He wanted to take a selfie with me and I said no. I didn't want anything on the internet. It was still a closed book that I was even talking to this person. He was a bit disappointed but I just framed it so that it seemed I just didn't want to have my picture taken.

He thought I was being an idiot.

"Why? You look amazing! You've worked so hard on your body and you've told me you're so much happier about yourself but you don't want to take a picture with me?"

"It's not that."

"It is that!"

"… it's not."

"Fine."

He wasn't in a shitty mood or anything, but I knew how fucking stubborn and short this man was and he just wasn't presenting the shitty mood, but I could tell it did hurt him. I just didn't want to be caught out for hanging out with someone I KNEWWW I shouldn't be giving the time of day to.

We went from dinner and walked all the way two suburbs away to a bar for drinks. K had called one of his friends that lived nearby to come and join us. I hadn't met this friend, I didn't even know what this friend knew about me.

We met him at the bar, a bar I'd never gone to before but because of the pandoodle, not many bars were left open.

I could feel K's entire demeanour change. All of a sudden went from a non-date, to walking to the bar holding hands, to him putting on a face in front of his friend acting like him and I were just friends. Sitting at an awkward distance, talking about me like we barely knew each other. Trying to impress his friend that frankly, I didn't give two fucks about if he liked me or not.

The drinks with his friend were awkward but it got to the point it was time to leave. We all walked to the train station. His friend walked off because he lived close enough he could just walk home. K was getting on the train and I was going to jump into a taxi.

His friend left, it was just K and I on the road talking a bit. He said he had to go, gave me a huge hug, said congratulations again, grabbed my face and before I had even a second to pull away he gave me a huge kiss on the lips. I couldn't escape it. But I didn't want to. I knew it was wrong, but it was a second. What the fuck did it mean?

I got in the taxi fucking confused, and slightly drunk. I didn't know what that meant, if it meant anything, but all I knew was it was fucking confusing. What was tonight? Like what the actual fuck was it?

So I got home and texted him and picked a fight. Of course. Destruction. Ruin the evening. Called him out for kissing me and manipulating me.

I went to sleep furious. I kept waking up in the night thinking what the actual fuck. It didn't help that I was a bit drunk, especially when I woke up with a bad hangover the next day that made my skin want to crawl and bleed and cry.

I knew I couldn't see him again. I couldn't do it. The next few nights he would video call me and I wouldn't answer, but he also wouldn't follow up. I couldn't bear to look at him even if it was through just a screen. How dare he think kissing me on the lips would be acceptable after all the hurt he'd put me through. I was half angry at him for acting this way, but then the other half was fucking furious at myself for continuously putting myself in this situation with him. Whenever he called, I felt he was trying harder and harder to get closer to me and I finally knew I had to stop. We both kept avoiding saying what we wanted from each other.

I wanted to start this new job and just dive into it. And I did. It was good to put my brain into something again and focus. But I was still confused about everything with K.

What was even more frustrating was I was sick of feeling confused. Sick of wondering 'what if' or pondering every detail of every interaction I'd had with the boy. I was sick of my own brain saying, just go with it. If anything, the pandoodle actually made me start learning I needed to be more up front in saying what I wanted. My whole 'just go with it' mantra hadn't gotten me really anywhere but hurt in the past and I was growing sick of being hurt all the time. I knew when it came to any form of communication with K that I needed to be direct and say that I was confused and say what I wanted from him.

K kept trying to reach out to me. Never apologising, he rarely did that. But I knew I had to end it myself.

I ended it. Over a message again because I didn't want the answer back. I told him I couldn't just be his friend and he had to go out there and figure out what he wanted and if he was ever ready for whatever it was properly with me, maybe we'd speak again. I couldn't bear the idea of walking away, but I couldn't hide myself any more. I told him I could really fall for him and I needed to not get there before it was too late and any form of connection got fucking ruined.

I understand. Thank you for your message. I'm still not ready, but if I was ready, you would be the perfect boyfriend. There's no one else. But for now, I understand and respect this.

Fuck. You. That's it? Wait, I sent this so he wouldn't respond. But that's it? If I'm the perfect boyfriend so you say, why the fuck are you still not ready. I actually cannot even comprehend this whole concept of 'not being ready'. Like when is anyone ever ready for this kind of shit. How do you know? I surely don't know if I'm ready, but I'm willing to take the dive. I don't fucking understand.

Fuck, you wasted my fucking time, again.

Damien

After K had been removed from the picture, I went back to focusing on work. October 2020, focussing on me. I felt like I'd said that literally every fucking year of my entire life.

And who was the perfect person to message when I was ferociously single? Damien.

Damien and I started speaking again and not long after that, we got back into our swing of things, and whenever I wanted something that felt like something, there he was.

Post K, it kind of occurred to me after a while that I had been treating Damien exactly like K had been treating me. So was I the fucking piece of shit in this situation? Probably. But we kept it going for a while longer.

2021 comes around, New Year – new… well fuck it, it's the same old me I don't need to change this year, I already lost 10+kgs during 2020. I was new enough.

Damien was coming over more frequently. Not staying the night because he said he didn't want to have his feelings hurt and he knew the situation I'd just come out of with K, but this time we actually spoke about what we both wanted from each other, and I think we were both on the exact same playing field.

We would spend hours talking about everything. It was nice having someone again who I could just talk to about all of my problems but at the same time, this time, not feel any emotional attachment to them. I could feel though that it would have to end at some point so I wouldn't hurt him. He was such a close friend to me by this point, not just because the sex was fucking mind blowing, but we spoke about everything.

EVERYTHING!

Could I date this guy? Absolutely not. Did I wish I could because it would be so fucking easy because he's right there? I fucking wish! But something was telling me that I just wasn't interested in him like that, and it was true, I wasn't.

A few months roll by. It's about April 2021 by this point. Damien and I had been doing our thing for months now, but I could feel it coming to an end. The times spent together were spreading further apart. We weren't chatting deeply any more. The arrangement was becoming very transactional. I don't know if it was me so much, but I know I was really chucking myself into work and trying hard to not waste anyone's time, especially my own now that I was finally busy again and free of the mental burden of K.

I remember in April 2021, the pan doodle kicked in heavily again. Sydney is going into another lockdown, this time a hard one. We were sent home extremely abruptly from work that day, all given masks to get home on the train.

It was getting a bit scary. No one knew what was going on, but we all kind of knew it was important to check in on each other.

A couple weeks had gone by, I'd texted Damien to check in and make sure he was OK. I didn't get a response. I didn't think anything of it, it was a fucking shit time for all of us at that point. We didn't know what was going on, we were only allowed at a 10km radius of our homes. It was fucked.

These next few weeks were really hectic weeks. Work was crazy. If anything, a lockdown made my workload get heavier as I worked in advertising production for a major supermarket. I was too busy to even think let alone check in on everyone, but these next few weeks, I couldn't predict how emotional I was going to be. I wish I'd known ahead of time, but there was no way to know.

Andrew

We were at a point where we were getting all our information from our phones.

Everyone's posting on their social media stories like there was literally not going to be a tomorrow. Posting about the news. Posting about whatever TikTok recipe they'd made that day. It was usually all fucking feta pasta at that point or loaves of bread. I didn't make any of them but had all of them still saved on my phone.

I would end up doom scrolling my life away as much as I possibly could purely to bypass the time. We all were. I was still living alone, so I really didn't want my brain being preoccupied by a man or anything I couldn't mentally handle. I needed content. All of the content.

I was watching someone's story and they'd posted a news article.

Gay couple fight in Sydney and ends in Murder.

I HAD to open it, and thank god I did, but also fuck my life why did I open that article.

I recognised the two guys mentioned in the article. I recognised the guy who'd murdered his partner. And I recognised the guy who was murdered.

The guy who murdered the other, I knew. We'd met up once to hook up, but I wasn't feeling it that night. We made out a little bit and I sent him home. He always messaged me wanting me but I just wasn't feeling it, and thank fuck I didn't that night because look at the outcome.

The guy who was murdered… I also had spoken to on apps, but never met up with. But I also knew him for another reason but it took me a minute to put the pieces together.

It was Andrew's ex from years ago.

My heart sank.

I hadn't spoken to Andrew since mid-2019. He was so bad at posting anything on social media. I didn't even know what was going on with him at all. He never used it and when he did it was just to post some stupid thing about how we didn't know what was in the vaccine. I had to play dumb to those things.

I formed a text that simply said something along the lines of,

I don't know if you've seen this yet or not, if not I'm so fucking sorry, if you have then I'm here if you need to talk but I couldn't see this without checking in on you. Again, if you haven't seen it, and this is how you're finding out, this makes me feel sick to my stomach but again, I'm here if you need someone to talk to, and attached the link.

I didn't know how to hit send. I felt like I could vomit everywhere. But I really couldn't not send it.

I hit send.

Within seconds the message was opened and I could feel my stomach go inverted.

I put my phone away for five minutes until I heard the message come back.

I hadn't seen it but thank you so much for sending it through to me. I need to process this. Thank you for the support, you don't need to do that but the fact that you are, is amazing.

Please, please, please, call me if you need anything. I don't know if you still live in the same flat or if you've moved but I don't care, if you need anything please let me know.

Thank you, I need to process this, we'll talk tomorrow

I felt fucking disgusting. I had just told my ex or whatever he was, that HIS ex from before me... had been MURDERED. Yes. This is real. This really happened. What the actual fuck is going on.

I called Noni to tell her what I'd just gone through just to inform her, and she was literally like, "Morgan, what the fuck is going on in the world?" It made me laugh, which is a little bit fucked in hindsight, but I kind of needed a moment of dark laughter. Laughter was all we really had during lockdown.

Andrew called me the next day. It was the first time I'd heard his voice in roughly two years. It was strange. Someone who I felt I knew so well at one point in my life yet when hearing his voice after so long it was as if I didn't recognise it. We spoke for a little bit and he said he'd really like to see me just for the company and comfort of someone listening to him. I said, it was absolutely fine. I realised at that moment I still cared for the guy. Sure, not in the same way I once did, but I cared to make sure he was OK.

He still lived in the same apartment which was only a five minute drive from me so I was more than OK with it. I felt being the person to break that kind of news to him that it was my duty to make sure he was properly OK and taking care of him, especially given the circumstances of the country at that moment.

Andrew came over the following night. It was nice to see him. He'd changed so much, he said I'd also changed so much and I'd grown up. By this point how old am I... twenty eight? Yep twenty eight!

He just came over to my apartment. It was a new place to what he'd last been to, so it was a little uncomfortable, besides the fact that it'd been two years. We just hung out and ordered take away food and talked for hours.

We actually, eventually, spoke about what had happened since. I'd told him all about K and the mental nightmare that he is. He told me about the boy he was seeing after me. I found it funny because the age difference between Andrew and I was a problem for us then, yet this boy was even younger than I was. We both spoke about a lot with each other and helped each other navigate the next parts. He was still stuck in his nightmare but I wasn't, but life in general had become a nightmare. It was a lockdown. He really shouldn't have even been over to begin with but it seemed we both needed the support.

We ended up talking about our situation. What went wrong, what really went down. We both let it all out, well after we'd both digested it.

He brought up that he was under the impression that he thought I never ever wanted a relationship with him after I rejected him in the hotel room. I told him that it was situational. He hadn't thought about the fact that he still lived with his ex and I didn't want to start a relationship with someone whose ex-boyfriend was in the other room and how awkward that could have been for me. I also reminded him that I'd literally said that to him at that moment. Once I'd said that he really took it on and it was like he had a full flashback moment and realised it. He said after I'd essentially said no that he couldn't really remember and it was as if he'd blacked out. I could understand that because it was something I've caught myself doing in serious discussions with people before as well.

There was a lot we hadn't actually said to each other, but finally got out. It was refreshing because whilst it showed me I still cared for the guy, I didn't have romantic feelings for him. I was a little bit brutal in saying I definitely felt I was falling for him and hoping he'd ask me to be in a relationship again, however when I really thought deep down about us, I wasn't proud to go home and let my family know I'd found someone. They simply never knew of his entire existence. But it took us ending for me to come to that realisation. He didn't like that, but we laughed and both admitted we were lucky we didn't dive into a relationship because that would have been even worse to deal with together.

We were actually getting along. We both let out a lot of shit we had obviously held back and not thought about again. It was weirdly therapeutic to let it all out, even years later.

Andrew and I only saw each other again once after that. We went for a walk, which didn't last long as he complained the entire time. So I dropped him home.

We continued to speak for a bit. I needed to care for someone who was really going through mourning. But during this time I needed some support as well. I needed the support I was used to.

Damien

I messaged Damien again.

Hey! I haven't heard from you in ages and with everything going on I wanted to check in to see if you're OK? Xx

I put my phone down, time flew, no reply. I thought it was fucking weird.

I opened up the message a couple days later only to realise it's gone through as a text message, not an iMessage. Weird. It's always gone through as an iMessage... maybe he's going through a bit of a mental blip. That wasn't abnormal for him. I'll leave it. He'll get it eventually and let me know.

Another week went by. I started to get a bit paranoid. I remembered we used to use another social media app to talk sometimes. I messaged him there and again, put my phone away. He's fine, nothing's happened, you're just paranoid.

A couple more days went by, still nothing from Damien. I kept forgetting and remembering later on. There was just A LOT going on at that time for really there not being anything going on at that time. We were in lockdown, nothing was going on but so much was going on.

I checked the message on the other platform. Unopened. What the actual fuck was going on?

I felt I was being ignored.

I left it another week. By this point, I was sick of being ignored. It's been weeks now and he'd never acted like this with me. Even the times he'd gone through a little bit of a mental breakdown, he'd still talk to me and reassure me that he was actually OK. I was really starting to worry about the guy. I missed him. I needed to make sure he was OK.

The paranoia kicked in full force. Knowing he had had mental health problems in the past and spoken so deeply about it, I started getting really worried.

I tried to call him.

"I'm sorry, this phone number has been disconnected."

What...

What the actual... fuck.

I had no idea where this man could be. I checked the other social media platform. Message still unopened.

His phone number was no longer in use. He was unresponsive on another form of contacting him. I have no idea how to get in contact with this person I cared deeply for.

I didn't know any of his friends. I don't think he really even had that many. I didn't know any of his family. His Facebook had been deactivated. I had nothing. No way to contact him.

I started to spiral.

Sitting on the couch by myself alone in my apartment thinking, *Oh my god, my friend could be dead and I have no idea how to find out.* I literally was going crazy. I called Noni and she talked me through calming down, but it wasn't working. I was on the phone to her saying all these outlandish thoughts about him being dead whilst pacing up and down my hallway. She could tell by my tone of voice I was full on spiralling. She knew I'd been trying to contact him for about a month now and even after hearing the thought that I was actually imagining him being dead she was really worried about me.

I opened my laptop and got on google. I started googling his first and last name followed by 'news'. Nothing came up to do with him.

I changed 'news' to 'obituaries'. Nothing. Thank god.

I couldn't find anything on the internet telling me someone by that name had died. But I was still left sitting there freaking out going *what the fuck has happened to him.* I was full-on panicking by this stage.

Then, I remembered a detail out of nowhere. We had the same middle name.

I changed the google search to his first, middle and last name followed by 'news' and all of a sudden, there was a hit.

All of a sudden, in a blink of an eye, I actually wished he had died...

There it was, first article on the internet.

Damien _____ _____ charged with child grooming offenses.

I didn't know how to process this. Someone I cared for has done this. Is this real? I opened the article and was reading. Freaking out as I read. This wasn't him. It couldn't be. There were pictures with someone's blurred face in the images. Then, there was the fourth image... confirmed. It's him.

I knew that tattoo on his shoulder. That's him. This is all him. This is real. I couldn't comprehend it. I was spiralling out of control.

I screenshotted it. Called Noni and she picked up and I simply said, "I found him."

She panicked and I said, "Check your messages." I texted her the screenshot of the article.

"Oh... my... god."

We both were just in disbelief. Noni was worried I was going to lose my mind and go into a total state of shock. I didn't know what to do next. I was in shock. I blacked out. I remember Noni talking to me just making sure I didn't lose it but I don't remember a thing. I can't remember a thing. I honestly don't recall what was said after that point. All I know is I went from walking up and down my hallway to sitting dead still on the couch and kept going back and forth from doing that for hours.

I eventually got off the phone from Noni. I kept walking back and forth in the apartment. In absolute disgust, I was thinking how the fuck could this have happened. I was recounting the last times I had seen him. I last saw him in April. I kept reading the article. The article was from the end of April.

This would have happened a week or two after I'd just seen him.

Your brain goes to some really dark places when something fucked up happens. But I'd never experienced my brain going somewhere as dark as this. I started recounting everything he'd ever said to me. Nothing added up. Nothing spelt out what he'd be caught doing. I couldn't think of anything.

Caught trying to seduce a thirteen-year-old boy.

This just kept replaying in my head over and over. Other friends, I talked to about this over the next few days, kept making really crude jokes like, "Well, I guess that means you look young," and other things like that but that made me feel even sicker. Sure, I'd giggle in the moment, but when left alone with my thoughts it made me feel disgusted.

Was he only doing what he was doing with me because I looked young? Was I fulfilling something within him that when I couldn't be around any more for one or two FUCKING WEEKS he felt the need to go to THAT level?

Was he so lonely he went down that route? Was it something he was always contemplating? Or was it something he was pursuing all along?

Where did I fall? What was my worth? How could I ever trust someone ever fucking again after finding this all out?

I just told someone WEEKS ago that their ex had been MURDERED and now I'm dealing with this? Someone I cared so deeply for being put in jail for attempted child grooming?

A paedophile?

I didn't really have anyone I could talk too deeply about it besides Noni. I would go for my 1 to 2 hour walks every single day and call her and just be talking about how I didn't know if I could trust someone ever again. She was the only person who would actually listen to me without making a sick joke about the whole thing. She'd let me spiral over the phone and just keep saying, "Get it out, keep talking," and at the end, I'd be exhausted from overthinking it.

I really struggled for a long time. Living alone during a state-wide lockdown, I felt I had no one. The apps before this were a fucked up sense of comfort in that when I felt down I could rely on some stranger I'd never met, and because of the lockdown, I didn't know when or if I'd ever meet them, but I could rely on them to give me a compliment or tell me they wish they could meet me. All of that comfort, I'd temporarily been fulfilling myself with using dating apps, was all of a sudden tainted... again... because who the fuck in this world can I trust?

If someone I cared for that much could go and do something like that... I can't... I couldn't stop thinking about it all. Was it happening whilst we were doing whatever it was we were doing?

Was it happening all this time? When did this all begin?

I woke up weeks later realising I had to stop thinking like this. I couldn't keep driving myself insane.

I would go for weeks checking if the message had ever been opened. It never was. That was how I knew he was still locked away. For charges like that I knew he wouldn't be released on bail. No fucking way. No chance. Would I ever know if he died there? I was coming to terms with the fact if anything happened to him inside jail that I may never know.

I can't think like that. I can't. It had to end.

And who was it to pop up out of nowhere to check in on me when I was spiralling out of control one night...

K

Hi, I just wanted to check in on you. I know you're living alone during lockdown so I wanted to say hi.

I read the message. I didn't open it for two hours. It had completely directed my mind elsewhere from Damien. All of a sudden I was freaking out about something else. It was kind of nice in a really fucked up way. All the problems with K were fucking miniscule in comparison to the drama of Damien.

Right at the moment, I needed this. Despite growing to hate K for the mental damage he'd done to me, I needed the distraction.

About 2 hours later, I video called him. I needed comfort.

He picked up within one ring.

"Hi!"

"Hey."

"I didn't expect you to respond, let alone call!"

"I honestly don't know why I'm calling."

I did.

"How are you? Are you OK?"

"Yeah I'm OK."

"... really?"

"... no."

"What's going on? Is it just hard being on your own?"

"Yeah it's partly that. I got some really fucked up news about a friend though."

"What's happened."

"I don't really want to talk about what's happened. I just want to try and forget about it for now if that's OK?"

"Don't worry, whatever's happening with your friend I'm sure it will work out."

"Don't."

"What?"

"This isn't something I want to work out. I hope it doesn't work out. It's really bad and I'm not going to tell you what happened, but the thing didn't happen directly to me, but basically I just want him to completely disappear."

"Oh, wow. I've never heard you talk about anyone like this."

"Yeah I know. I've never talked about anyone like this before."

"Really... are you OK?"

"No. I'm really not."

"What can I do?"

"Distract me and make me laugh, or try to."

K, then just made a bunch of stupid faces on the screen. Something he'd often do to make me laugh back when we'd video call when we were good. It didn't make me laugh, but I did eventually smile just a smidge.

He loved that little smile.

We kept speaking for an hour or so. He gave me that little bit of comfort I needed at that exact moment. He was the last person I'd expect to contact me, but I was happy he did at that moment. My brain was telling me shit like, *It's like he knew I needed help,* but all of it was just dumb luck.

K for the next few weeks would message me and check in every single day. And I mean it. Every. Single. Day. He also called every couple days. It meant a lot considering everything that had been going through my head.

It didn't make me start swooning again. It gave me comfort that someone was caring about me and really checking in on me. Especially during a time when we really needed people to check in especially on our single friends who lived alone. Something a lot of my friends tended to forget as they lived with their flatmates or boyfriends or girlfriends. Whilst we were all alone in lockdown, I was literally alone.

But in a sense... I had K.

I knew I couldn't get too comfortable. I knew the time would come where we wouldn't speak. He wasn't working because of the lockdown. I knew he'd get busy and would return to work. And that's exactly what happened.

Another month went by and we all of a sudden weren't speaking any more. And that was fine. I didn't swoon. I'd gotten comfortable knowing he'd reach out. But I have comfort as well in the fact that we both know we shouldn't continue, especially after what we'd been through.

By this point, it was maybe October 2021. Everything was going OK, I was looking to move as my lease was coming to an end and so was lockdown and I needed a new start.

James, Kevin and Jeff

November 2021, I'm moving to a new area.

A new start, lockdown was kind of over, we were able to go out and do things again, and I was ready to really embrace a new area and a new start. I'd moved not far from where I was, but enough that it felt like a fresh place. Somewhere I didn't have any bad memories of and somewhere I didn't feel stuck at home. Somewhere I could go out and explore and see a new bunch of shit. This was good for me.

And better than that, a new area for me to swipe left and right on men… or fuck boys… that's to be confirmed.

I'd matched with a lot of new guys in the area. I was talking to everyone. They were all thinking I'd just moved interstate and new to the entire city as we'd been stuck inside swiping on the same guys for so many months now. I matched with a bunch, a few I'd end up hanging out with.

James, Kevin and Jeff were the ones I'd end up seeing.

James was lovely, very quiet, but most importantly, horrified that I'd never finished the Harry Potter books or movies. He clung onto it and I saw it as an opportunity to bond. We'd go for dinners and hang out at each other's houses and he insisted that we watch the movies. He hated the fact I hadn't finished them. Also hated the fact that since the pandemic started, it was something on my To-Do list that I still hadn't completed and only ever got up to the fourth movie. We started from the first one because he wanted me to have the FULL experience.

By the second movie… I was ready to sleep with him. I was doing all the moves, wanting it, kissing him, it was very PG13 though. He liked kissing and cuddling, which was cute, but after a couple weeks of hanging out I was literally thinking, *Is he more interested in Harry Potter or me?*

I'd stay over, hoping he'd initiate sex. I tried, but it didn't translate. I didn't know what was going on. It was kind of playing with my confidence, because I dunno if it was lockdown that had made me feel so out of the game or what, but I'd never had this problem with getting laid before. All he wanted to do was cuddle.

By a couple of weeks later, we'd made it to the fourth movie. At this point we've been hanging out for about a month. I'd given up on trying to get laid by this guy who only wanted to peck me and cuddle me at night. Maybe lockdown made him so lonely that's all he was wanting. But like… lockdown just made me extremely horny, so what the fuck was I going to do. We finished the movie and went to bed. Nothing happened. I fell asleep in seconds and the next morning I just went home. We spoke a bit after that but then I was literally exhausted at the idea of seeing another one of those movies and not getting anything out of it that I couldn't be bothered with it all any more.

Was that fucked? Probably, but I didn't care. Lockdown taught me we really don't have time to waste, and I'd realised I was wasting my time.

I'd literally been cock-blocked by Harry Potter, and the annoying thing isn't just that I didn't even get laid once by someone I liked, but we got to the fourth movie… which before James, that's where I was already fucking up to. Didn't even get to see any new content out of all of this shit!

About a week later, I matched with Kevin.

Kevin was nice with a very dark sense of humour which I liked. Almost very masculine minded which I'd never spoken to someone almost so masculine it was different for me.

He was very sexually minded as well. Messages were really kinky, not my taste but fun to message back to I guess.

After the sexual tension built up and went nowhere with James, Kevin's mindset was kind of what I was craving.

We hung out, made out a lot, sex didn't get there but I was at a mental place where I didn't wanna just give it to everyone like I was used to doing. I wanted to at least get to know someone first before diving into bed with them. The damage from K and Damien led me to being in this mindset. Don't give it to them straight away. Let them earn it. You're worth more than that.

Kevin and I started talking pre-Christmas. During Christmas he went out of town and back to where he was from. We spoke everyday, almost all day long.

He used an app mainly for communication, one that I didn't really use any more. One that still had a message unopened from Damien...

What I didn't know at that time was that the app allowed you to see the person's location if they had their location settings on. I didn't even know mine were on.

Kevin over the course of time would send me lots of messages there. What I didn't know was he was watching my every move. He'd know when I was home. He'd know where I was when I was hanging out with friends. He made a comment saying, "Oh, you're a north shore boy," when he knew I was seeing my parents at their house for the day. It didn't even occur to me that he'd figured that out as I didn't know these location settings were even turned on.

I'd go to the supermarket and he'd message me saying something like , *Are you buying me orange juice?*

Weird.

There was one day we went to hang out come January 2022. I really wanted to go to the beach but to a different beach. He lived not far from some beaches I hadn't really explored before so he said to pick him up and we'd go for a swim.

We did that. By this stage, I'd gotten more and more comfortable with him despite not knowing about the whole location thing. We'd been sleeping at each other's apartments, making out heaps. We'd done some sexual stuff but not the full deed. It was cute, I'd say we were seeing each other.

But this day at the beach really spelt out to me that there was something up…

I was lying there, tanning oil, sunscreen, in my tiny little speedo, since now I was thin, I felt beautiful and confident. He then made a comment that felt really strange.

"You look so gay today."

"… what?"

"Your little speedo."

"… what's that supposed to mean."

"Nothing it's just a joke."

"I don't get it."

I kept lying there tanning.

I got up and went to go into the water, asked, "If he wanted to come in."

He said, "Nah."

I walked down and went into the water, had a few minutes

cooling off, and a couple minutes to spiral about what he'd just said. I don't really understand how someone wearing just a speedo could 'look so gay'. I knew he had this hyper-masculine mind-set but it made me feel weird all of a sudden. Maybe because in my life I often forget I am even gay. It's been such a normal thing for me as I've been gay my whole life and out of the closet for half of my life. It wasn't something I really even thought about any more because no one in my life ever made me feel different for being gay. But that comment, even coming from a gay man, made me feel different again.

I got out of the water and walked back up to Kevin and lay back down.

"You look like a bond girl coming out of the water."

I laughed but he wasn't laughing.

"What do you mean?"

"The way your hips go side to side, the strut."

"Did I do that?"

"Yeah it was funny, so gay."

"… OK, that's weird."

"What's weird?"

"You've called me gay twice now and I just don't get what

you mean by that."

"Oh sorry, I just say it sometimes."

"I just don't get it. It's a bit redundant of a word to use to describe someone if it's not used to literally describe their sexuality."

"Nah, don't worry."

"OK."

We kept lying there in the sun, it was boiling but it was still nice.

We chatted a bit, he was being cute again, it was back to the flirty conversation that I liked.

I leant in at one point maybe half an hour later to kiss him. He leant away and went;

"Dude, no homo."

"Excuse me?"

"I don't need everyone here knowing I'm gay."

"…"

"Nah, seriously."

"… they already know."

"Nah."

That made me feel extremely uncomfortable. Like I wasn't allowed to kiss the guy I'd been kissing all the time in public. Like I had to shelter myself for someone when I'd lived in the closet the first half of my life. I was so uncomfortable with it. It really turned me off.

I don't think after that we really spoke about anything. Just lay there in silence waiting for someone to suggest leaving.

I eventually suggested packing up and heading off. We got up and headed back to the car.

"I'm gonna drop you home then I have some stuff to do tonight and I'm seeing a friend after that."

"Oh, you're not coming over?"

"Nah, I've got stuff I need to get done."

"Really?"

"Yeah, I just said that."

This was a lie. We sat in silence as I kept driving. He'd turned me off with the whole 'no homo' shit so much I just wanted to drop him home and escape.

I dropped him off. He gave me a mad attitude and slammed my car door. I was a bit in shock. He was acting like a baby because I wouldn't come inside.

I drove home and sat on my couch.

He messaged me on the app. Sent some sad picture that he was bored because I ruined his afternoon.

I opened it and didn't respond.

He messaged me saying, *You're home?*

Yep.

So, you don't have other things to do?

I have things to do at home.

Sure.

I didn't reply then. It was getting annoying and childish. Sure, I should have been honest, but it was as if he was having a temper tantrum that I had things to do. Even if they were fake, the attitude and response I was getting from him was totally immature.

I walked to the grocery store an hour later.

He messaged again, *What's doing?*

Just going to get groceries.

I can see that.

I SEE? At this moment, I was actually getting really concerned. Was I reading too much into things? But then… I saw my location's settings were on.

HE WAS FOLLOWING ME. It all clicked at that moment. He'd been following me on this app for weeks. Everything, EVERYTHING clicked in my mind.

I switched them off. He immediately noticed and I was getting an abundance of *where are you?* messages.

I didn't reply to any of them for the rest of the night.

Woke up the next day. More messages. By this stage I was so exhausted of feeling like I had to let someone who'd pissed me off know exactly where I was at every 20 minute interval of the day. I just didn't reply any more for the day.

A couple of days later, we spoke again. He wanted to see me. I wasn't sure I wanted to. It was really exhausting literally dealing with someone acting so clingy and needing to know my every move. I mean we'd probably hung out like five times and he was acting really possessive over me.

I'd lied and said I had plans that Friday night and a friend was coming over. He suggested he come over after my friend left. I told him I was hanging with my friend and wasn't going to kick them out by a certain time so he could come over and that I'd let him know what time if I could be bothered even seeing him by that stage.

I wanted a night to myself. Just to chill. It'd been a hectic week with work and I wanted to sit on the couch and binge TV and eat crap food and just chill.

He messaged every 30 minutes asking if my friend had left yet.

This just made me even less likely to want to spend time with him. It got to about 10p.m. and I messaged him, *My friend's still here but probably leaving in an hour and then I'm just going to go straight to bed so we'll talk tomorrow.*

I got an abundance of messages, almost begging me to let him come over. I don't know what was going on with him but it was a lot. It got to about 11p.m., I opened the messages, and I'd had enough.

You don't seem to respect the fact that I'm hanging out with my friend! You're almost pressuring me to ask them to leave so you can have me! I told you I was exhausted, we didn't have any plans I told you, I'd let you know but it wasn't likely to happen.

He opened it, screenshotted it, and didn't reply.

I went to bed and slept like a fucking baby that night. I felt relaxed for finally saying my mind and giving it back to him. The way he was acting was so childish. I just needed him to leave me be for a moment.

The next day, he messaged me like nothing had happened. Like I hadn't called him out on his behaviour.

I ignored it.

Ten messages later, no acknowledgement of his behaviour, I'd had enough.

You never even acknowledged my message about how intense you were last night. That's why I haven't responded to you. You're ignoring what I said. No acknowledgment. No apology for your behaviour. You didn't seem to respect that I was busy and that I was exhausted. All you cared about was coming over despite how I felt. You track me with what I'm doing which is a major turn off and pretty fucked up. I'm sorry for ignoring you but frankly you pushed me to it considering I didn't wanna speak to you after how you carried on. I understand you like me but that's just not how you should behave. I think it's just done now.

I screenshotted it to read it when I wasn't intoxicated, but I couldn't find it. I am sorry. And sorry I made you feel that way. I do respect your other commitments even though it didn't show. I understand how you feel but I don't want it to be done Morgan. Can we meet up and speak about this? What can I do to make it up to you Morgan?

No, I don't think so. I think we should just leave it for now. I don't really have anything more to say cos I just don't have the energy for this any more. If something comes in the future it does, but as of right now you need to address this shit within yourself x.

Really? I think it's silly to just chuck it all away over a conversation. The last thing I wanted was to argue with you. I just really wanted to see you and I know you were busy and yes I did overreact. I'm sorry!

I get that. Thank you for apologising. Maybe in the future but for now let's just leave it. I'm never someone to cancel out any possibility, but when it's unbalanced like it is now, it's not healthy. So please just leave it for now. We'll speak soon. X

I wouldn't say unbalanced. I don't want to leave it because we will probably never talk again. I'm not the sort of guy to leave a situation when it's shit because that isn't healthy.

I didn't respond after that. He was trying to hold onto something that I was trying to let go of. Was it shitty that I didn't reply after that? Probably. But he had exhausted all the energy out of me. Kevin had actually started to scare me.

Over the next week, Kevin would bombard me with messages and pictures of himself. Telling me everything he was doing. Acting like I was asking what he was up to. I never replied.

There was one night, he messaged me with a pin to his location. He was on a walk in my suburb. It alarmed me… and about 20 minutes later, the buzzer for my apartment went off.

I didn't answer it. That scared the shit out of me. I wasn't expecting a friend, no food delivery, nothing. Whether it was him or someone else simply buzzing the wrong apartment number, I didn't answer it. I turned off the living room light and sat in my bedroom quietly for about 30 minutes. I didn't know what else to do.

The apartment block structure was racing through my mind. You needed to buzz the apartment number to get through the front door, but once you were in, you were in. You didn't need a buzzer or anything to use the elevator. I didn't have a little peep hole in my front door to see what was on the other side. And the apartment block alone had probably fifty apartments in it, so the front door was constantly being opened. In times where I'd stupidly left my keys inside just taking out the recycling, all I needed to do was wait up to 5 minutes for someone to come to the front door and let me in.

All these thoughts were racing through my mind. Was I being paranoid? I didn't even know if it was him!

It happened again the next night.

And the night after that.

I never replied to Kevin after that. I removed him from the app he'd message me mainly on. He'd message me on others but I just ignored them. There was nothing I could reply with that would make him stop. I had to ghost. I'd never been that person to just ghost someone before, but I was actually scared and whether it was him or not, my brain was only processing that it was him.

Kevin scared the shit out of me. It was only about a month or so that we were hanging out but that kind of possessiveness was something that freaked me out.

I didn't open a dating app or anything for weeks.

By this stage, it's maybe the end of January. I got a notification that someone liked me on a dating app. I ignored it for a day. Then opened it to see who this could be.

It was someone called Jeff. Cute, nothing special, nothing I immediately wanted to like back. However, I eventually did. I was still a little cursed from the Kevin debacle and maybe it would be nice to just speak to someone new.

I liked him back. He messaged me immediately. The conversation was super organic. Super chill. So easy. Fucking good banter!

I had plans to go up-state with Aileen for her birthday in a couple of weeks' time in mid Feb, so I knew I really only had a little bit of time if I wanted to meet Jeff before going away.

He wanted something chill. We planned to have lunch... but from the vibe of the banter we both couldn't wait.

He explained the complex hours of his job. He worked down the road from where I lived. He was being REALLY cute one night and I jokingly said, *You finished work at 5a.m. and that's perfect time to curl into my bed and cuddle me before I have to get up for my day.*

What's your address? I want to finish work and curl straight into you.

What the actual fuck. He took the bait! I was gonna go to bed comfortably without dealing with the awkward spooning arm whilst I'm trying to fall sleep and could just be woken up at 5a.m., open the door, curl back into bed half asleep and have someone just curl into me and spoon me exactly as I'm so fucking tired nothing could keep me awake.

Perfect.

I went to bed that night and woke up to a call at 5.15a.m. I buzzed him in. Let him inside. Went straight to bed, he curled up next to me and we went straight to sleep.

I woke up three hours later for work. The poor guy got three hours of sleep and I'm up and going, "OK, TIME FOR WORK," as if he'd had an equal amount of sleep to me.

I was oblivious to the fact he'd barely slept but he still got up. I told him to stay in bed and sleep as long as he wanted. I even brought my coffee and brought my work laptop into the bed and just sat next to him. He didn't want to sleep. He spooned my leg and lay there all adorable as fuck. It killed me. I immediately thought this was beautiful. This man literally is hugging my leg and letting me get on with my day. Disgusting. Why was my brain thinking like this? A few weeks ago if Kevin had done that to me I'd thought he was a clingy fuck.

But with Jeff it felt cute. It felt adorable. It was gentle and not riddled with doubt.

He eventually got up and said, "I'll leave you to work so I can go home and get a proper sleep," and grabbed my face and kissed me.

I went, "No, you can sleep here!" The second the words came out of my mouth, I thought, *Yuck, what the fuck, Morgan.*

He went, "No, I can't because I won't sleep. I'd just want to kiss you all morning."

And he kissed me again.

He left and I got to work. He texted me before he even got into the car.

That was completely worth it.

This became a routine for us almost every day over the next week. 5a.m. wake ups and cuddles and three hour sleeps and coffee in bed and hugging my leg.

I was almost annoyed that I was going away soon but I also needed the holiday.

Whilst I was away we spoke every single day. Non-stop. He kept saying cute things like he missed me. I was completely falling for it. Sending me cute selfies of him waiting for me to come home. Telling me he couldn't wait to take me on a proper date. Telling me he'd told his mum about me and she was already excited. His friends were excited. It was all a lot for someone I'd simply cuddled and kissed a few times before we'd even had a proper date, but all I can say is it was so nice.

I finally got home from my trip, excited to see him. I got home late and had to go to bed and he turned up as per usual at 5a.m. This time I jumped into his arms at the door and kissed him. He carried me to bed and we curled straight up and he kept kissing my neck and shoulders saying he missed me so much. I think both of us just really felt comfortable with each other and the connection was definitely taking over us.

The thought went through my mind that we were getting carried away with it all, but I really didn't give a fuck. I was going with it. Something I'd tried to do so many times with guys, but often failed.

But this time, I just kept telling myself, GO WITH IT.

He was the first guy in a long time where the connection felt like it was enough that I didn't need to lay everything I wanted on the table. He'd proved to me in telling his family and friends of my very existence that he wanted something more than just a cuddle. So my old mentality of 'just going with it' actually felt right at this moment.

The next week both of our jobs had crazy busy weeks coming up. We tried to spend as much time together as we could.

He finally invited me over to his for the night. I couldn't stay over as I had a meeting earlier than my start time with the CEO and my boss the next day.

We had dinner, curled up on the couch, watched TV, spoke for hours and laughed at literally everything. He couldn't take his hands off me, constantly playing with my hair, my ears, kissing my neck, it was fucking cute. It was a really nice night. I wish I could have stayed.

The next day, I got to work early for the meeting, only to find out the meeting had been cancelled.

I immediately texted him saying, *I'm so annoyed because if I'd known earlier I could have stayed the night!*

His tone after that changed. I think he thought I was gaslighting him or lying about ever having the meeting. But after that he wasn't the same.

Over the next few weeks, I tried speaking to him and planning to go out for dinner. I always got excuses that work was crazy, then I'd get love bombing messages that would soon stop. I was being gaslit. Something had turned him off that was out of my control.

I started to question everything about myself. Really pushing my self-confidence down. Why had I gotten so swooned by this guy and felt this connection so strong then it just overnight switched. Something I was so fucking used to. Guys switching off on me out of absolutely nowhere.

I didn't hear from him for two days. This in hindsight isn't that long, but really, it's ages when you're as anxious of a person as I am.

I went to bed one night and was hoping to hear from him. As I'm just drifting off I see my phone light up and hear the ding.

How have you been?

No. Not from Jeff, It was K, at 2.14a.m. Fuck off.

I ignored it and went to sleep.

I woke up the next day having forgotten the message. Got up, made my coffee, sat on the couch then looked at my phone and saw the preview for the text again. What the fuck. What the actual fuck. I didn't open it for hours. When I finally opened it properly, I didn't know how to respond, so I didn't. I left him on read. I felt so smug that I had the ability to do that. To leave someone that hurt me so much on read. Whenever I thought about K, I was at the point where I didn't think of all the good times, I thought of all the hurt and misleading. And even when I thought about the good times, I didn't consider them good any more. I thought of them as the bare minimum, because that's what they were. The bare fucking minimum.

I couldn't leave the message on read for that long. Turns out my willpower wasn't that strong. That night I texted back.

Lol, 2a.m.?

Hey, I didn't expect you to respond at that time. I was heading home.

OK.

I know you didn't expect to hear from me but I was missing you and wanted to check in.

Why?

I just said it, I was missing you.

OK.

He didn't reply after that but my short *OK* message was meant to have that intention. Don't tell me you fucking miss me. This was his pattern.

The next night, I got another text from him.

Hey, I know my text was really out of the blue, but I didn't expect your response. It took me by surprise that you reacted that way. I thought we could always talk to each other. Anyways, I hope you've been well x.

It was at that moment, I could tell he was reaching out because he needed the support. Me, being someone who was too fucking caring with people I truly cared for, I couldn't just leave him sat there. I knew I needed to give him something, even if it was the bare minimum.

What's wrong?

I've been going through some shit and I missed you and wanted to talk but if you don't want to I understand.

What's wrong?

Some shit's been going on at home and I just wanted a friend to talk to.

Do I have to repeat myself a third time? What's wrong?

My grandmother died.

I immediately called him. He was OK. Like I've previously said, I'd been through death way too many times to count. A lot of my family is older than the normal of someone my age, so really I'd gone through lots of death which is not a great quality, but definitely something a lot of friends have turned to me in the past for advice on. We spoke for a while. I was concerned especially for him as he lived overseas from his entire immediate family. He wasn't able to go back for the funeral. He was just upset because he didn't know how to process it. It was the first death he'd been through. We eventually got off the phone and he texted me simply saying.

Thank you for calling me. I didn't expect you to do that for me, but I really appreciate you and what we talked about.

I didn't respond. I thought the call was enough. Don't get me wrong, his message was lovely, but I didn't think it needed to be replied to any further.

The next day, I heard from Jeff, *I'm sorry, I haven't been very communicative. I'm just going through some shit and I really just need time.*

Are you OK?

I'm OK. I'm just sorry I can't be with you right now.

Fuck. Another done. Another switched off out of nowhere.

What's wrong? What happened?

I don't really want to talk about it if that's OK. You're amazing. We'll talk soon.

Done. Over. Finito. So much for that fresh start…

K

I checked in on K a couple of days later because, fuck my life, why do I have to be this person that fucking CARES! I wish, I could possess the power that the men I seem to attract have where they can just fucking switch off, but I don't have that power...

Let me know if there's anything you need. I'm here if you want to talk.

I knew this was the fucking worst thing I could do, but after another rejection and switched off guy, I felt lonely. I knew this was such an unhealthy pattern within myself, but it was also a pattern for K and I. It sucks that something so horrific had to happen for him to reach out, but in a sick sense, I was happy he thought of me when push came to shove.

K asked, if he could video call me. I said sure.

We spoke over the phone for hours that night about everything. Career, future, marriage perspectives, children perspectives, everything really except for us and our past connection which in that call I'd realised was still there. It'd probably always be there...

I think he called me around 9p.m. I was up talking to him on the phone till probably 1.30a.m. or 2a.m. I didn't want to get off the phone even though I had work the next morning, luckily from home that day, but still, I just couldn't get off the phone.

The conversation was probably the best it'd ever been. He told me he was finally interested in going freelance and opening his own business. I was mentally like GREAT, I know people who work in his field, I can ask around and find out rates and rental norms, just to help where I could.

I spoke to a few people randomly and got the stats. Screenshotted them and sent them to him. He was incredibly grateful and thankful that I'd gone out of my way to ask around for information that could help his career.

We got to a point where he was video calling me every single day. It went on for a couple of weeks. I would finish work and get excited for him to call, and he would, like clockwork.

It was becoming the best part of my day.

A couple weeks went by, it's maybe March 2022 by this point and my brain was starting to completely spiral about him. He called one night and I didn't answer. 20 minutes later, he texted me.

No call?

A little psycho bit of rage and spite came over me.

I'm not your boyfriend, we don't need to call every day.

OK

I felt powerful. But I also felt like an absolute dick. It wasn't like me to talk like this. It was more like me to be on the other side of this. But for some reason it really did feel powerful.

The next day, I had a really good day, killed it at work, finished a gigantic project, and felt super empowered from the day. I got home from work and expected his call, but when K didn't call like clockwork I was confused. It was as if I'd forgotten that the night prior I had been a complete dick to him. I think I blacked it out of my memory because it wasn't something I'd usually do to someone I cared about.

Fuck it, I'll call him. He answered but was confused why I'd called him.

"I thought you didn't want to talk any more."

"No it's just literally what I said, I'm not your boyfriend, so really do we have to speak everyday? It's fine to miss a day!"

"OK, good, I was confused and didn't want that to just be the end of our conversations."

I was really grasping at straws because I really wanted to stick it to him by proving a point, but in reality I wanted to speak to him every day. Every single day. Oh fuck, what have I started. I realised just then that I'd become reliant on him again. But it was like an addiction, I needed the connection. I needed his connection.

We kept speaking over the phone every night. Usually for a minimum of an hour, sometimes four.

One weekend, he messaged me asking what I was up to that night. I was kind of over sitting at home waiting for his calls so I told him I had no plans. He simply messaged saying,

Video call tonight?

Do we always have to do a video? It's Saturday night after all.

I could tell from his response he was a bit shocked. I'd said that. The fact that I'd suggested something not via a phone, it sent him.

Well, we could hang out if you wanted? I didn't think you wanted to though.

I'm down, could just do dinner or something.

OK cool! I finish work at 5.30 so do you want to meet somewhere around 7?

I could just meet you at your work?

That'd be good then we can spend more time together.

Fuck. Had I just made plans to hang out with K in person for the first time in a year and a half? We'd spoken a lot over that time, but it's always different in person. Was the connection still there in person as it was over the phone? I guess I'll find out in a matter of hours...

The drive over to his work (remember, still 20 kms away) my head kept spinning. What the actual fuck was I doing. Why was I doing this to myself again? Why was I literally throwing myself into the lion's fucking mouth? Why are you such a shit person Morgan? Why! I was spiralling. Calm down. It's just dinner. YEAH BUT IT'S DINNER WITH THE MAN WHO RUINED YOU. Nope, it's just dinner. IT'S JUST DINNER.

I turned up to his work, he was finishing up with a client so I waited out the front.

He texted me saying, *Finished! Where are you?*

I got up and walked in, he was on the work phone finishing up. We both smiled HUGE as we saw each other and I sat in the waiting seats as he wrapped up. It was the first time I'd seen this man's face in person in over a year. Fuck, he was still cute.

He was still on the phone and walked over to me and grabbed my head. Weird. First touch. Then he used his hand to lift my chin so he could look at my eyes and we both smiled. He went back to the desk and wrapped up the call. Put the phone down, walked over to me, went 'stand up'. I stood up and he gave me the biggest hug. It would have been a solid 7 seconds, felt like 2 minutes, but it was comforting and just like the hugs I remembered.

I realised, I was nervous.

The conversation flowed naturally, but I was still nervous and anxious around him. He was unpredictable, or maybe we were unpredictable. I didn't expect my heart to beat as fast as it did but seeing him and having that sense of touch from him again, immediately all the good came back to me.

We hopped in my car and started driving. We didn't actually know where we were going yet, but the conversation was electric and neither of us could stop. Just laughing. I'd missed laughing with him. FUUUUCK. He said he wanted to get changed first because he felt gross from the work day so we drove to his place.

I'd never seen inside his apartment before. He'd moved, this time he wasn't living with his family any more but he was living with two friends. A three bedroom apartment. It was in the next suburb from where I grew up so I knew the area like the back of my hand already. There was a weird comfort in that.

We went into his room, I schlepped onto his bed and just sat on my phone. He proceeded to get undressed and I said, "Oh, do you want me to wait in the living room so you can get dressed?"

"Morgan, it's not like you haven't seen any of this before. Just stay."

I locked my eyes onto my phone to pretend I wasn't looking in my peripherals. He fully just got naked in front of me and started asking me what I thought he should wear. Completely naked, showing me shirts and pants. I kept being like 'just wear black' and not looking away from my phone. He was testing me to try and make me look. I wasn't budging.

He got dressed and we left for dinner. Back in the car, electric conversation, laughter, we drove a couple suburbs to find a restaurant. Something easy. We always ate sushi together, so of course we ended up at a sushi restaurant. We walked around, he tried to hold my hand a couple times but I kept withdrawing. All the while the conversation and laughing never ended. It was organic. Nothing was ever forced with us.

After a couple of hours and several deep conversations, we hopped back in the car and I dropped him home. I was parked in the basement of his apartment block. When saying goodbye from my car, I think we both didn't know what to do. Kiss on the cheek? Awkward hug? I parked the car and I could tell he was trying to keep the conversation moving. But it was 10p.m. and I had to drive 30 minutes to get home. Get out of my car K!

He leant in and gave me a really awkward hug, but then again, I didn't know if it was awkward because we both didn't want to say goodbye or why it was awkward.

He got out of the car and I drove off. He waved from the distance, I could see in my rear view mirror.

I was maybe 10 minutes driving home and he called me. I answered.

"Hey, what's wrong? Did you leave something in the car?"

"Nothing's wrong, I just thought I'd call you and we could talk for your drive home."

We spoke the entire way home, then I parked and went upstairs and we kept speaking over the phone for another couple of hours. It was about 1a.m. by the time we finally got off the phone and finished the conversation.

I was definitely reading too much into everything. But he was also leaning into it all. I didn't know what was going on but the fact we'd finally met up and hung out in person again meant something to me. It's like all this time hadn't passed and we were fine, we were both right there.

The romantic side of me was thinking FINALLY. But reality kicked in and I realised I hadn't told one person that K and I had reconnected. I couldn't bear the idea of telling anyone. I wanted to go through this phase of him alone until I knew it was worth telling anyone. Maybe we'd end up dating. Maybe we'd just keep doing this thing. I didn't even realise I'd completely cut myself from any other connections from apps or men in my DMs and that I was giving all my time and energy to this man that I didn't know if he even wanted it or not. But then again, he was the one calling me every night. He was the one caring.

This gave me hope.

Over the course of the next few weeks, we were hanging out again in person probably twice a week, but it'd gotten to the point where sleepovers were happening. No kissing, no sex, but watching hours and hours of TV and laughing and picking on each other. He would put his arm around me and I would lie against him for hours. It was comfortable. It was what I'd gotten from other men, but this time from the man, I think I wanted all along.

When I looked at him I'd feel this comfort of knowing he wanted me. He'd smile at me for no reason and I'd catch him and he'd say things like, "I'm just happy you're here again."

Fucking. SWOON.

We'd fall asleep spooning. He'd be playing with my hair and back and kissing my shoulders. I could feel him against me, definitely comfortable.

One night, the spooning got physical and the next thing we were making out for hours. He suggested having sex and reality kicked in for us both when I said, "No, we're not dating, I'm not giving you that again unless it's real." He laughed but I was serious, but of course we kept making out.

Eventually, we had to stop because if I'd kept going I would have given in. The way we kissed was electric. It was familiar because well, it wasn't our first rodeo. I was hooked. We eventually went to sleep.

I woke up the next morning smitten as fuck. I woke up to kisses from him on my back, curling in tighter as he spooned me, and the perfect first few words that I always wanted to be woken up to…

"Want me to make you a coffee?"

SMITTEN.

"You shouldn't even be asking, you already know the answer."

He went and made me a coffee and brought it to me in bed. We had our morning coffees and kissed a couple times. It was like an old married couple waking up in the morning. It was exactly the kind of morning I'd dreamt of. Perfect.

I had to drop him off at work, so we got ready, drove him to work, he ran in and bought me a takeaway coffee and I drove home. Smiling the entire drive home. S M I T T E N.

My mum called me on the drive home by chance. He lived in the same area that I grew up in and my parents still lived there. It's like she knew I was in the area. The Mum radar. I answered and she was surprised I was even awake at that time. It was maybe 9.30a.m. on a Saturday, and I caved. I told her I was just driving home. She was confused.

I said, "I've reconnected with a boy who lives near you and I'm really happy and everything is going amazing so far."

Mum being Mum, worried but also happy, she was nervous but also excited because I'd never really spoken to her about any man in my life.

I had plans to see K again that night when he finished work, so Mum told me to go over to hers in the afternoon, since I had to go back to that area anyway.

I went over and Mum got all the information out about K. She was excited but also after hearing that this was someone I'd not just revisited once, or twice, but well, who knows by now, she was very sceptical but didn't directly tell me, she would just say things like 'take it slow' and 'be careful'.

Mum, also being a Mum, asked me what to call him.

"So, is he your boyfriend?"

"No no, we're not there yet."

"But you're dating?"

"I don't even know if we're there yet."

"So you're friends?"

"Fuck no never call him that."

"So what the hell do I refer to him as?"

"Just… he's my K."

"I don't know what that means, Morgy."

"Neither do I."

We laughed.

K was about to finish work so I left my parents place to go get him. I would park the car and walk to the front of his work and wait for him to finish. Who the fuck am I? Why am I being like this? I have no idea, it just all felt different this time.

We jumped in the car, we didn't know what to do that night besides get dinner and watch TV cuddling in his bed. I told him that I'd told my mum of his existence. He was shocked. I told him the funny conversation that Mum didn't know what to call him. He didn't laugh like I was laughing.

"What do you even mean, we're just hanging out?"

Fuck.

"Yeah, but you're just you, that's all I told her."

"We're friends!"

"K, friend's don't do that."

"I mean sure but we're not even dating yet, she's getting a bit ahead of herself."

"Shut up, they're my parents they're meant to."

It went silent for a couple of minutes.

We got to his place and I could tell the energy was off. We

sat in bed, not connected to me, no arm around me, not touching me at all. We watched TV and eventually just went to bed. No spooning was involved. My anxiety got the better of me that night. I barely slept that night. I'd definitely said too much. I'd definitely gotten ahead of myself, but I also know that I'm not crazy for feeling what I felt. My mind was racing. I think we tried to go to sleep around 11 but my mind kept me wide awake thinking until probably 3a.m. He slept with ear plugs in so I knew the fidgety side of me could make the tiniest amount of noise. My brain was taking over, replaying every single thing and word that'd happened in the last 24 hours. I eventually fell asleep, but only because my brain had exhausted itself thinking for so long.

The next morning, we woke up and he still made me my morning coffee, but no sitting in bed and cuddling or kisses. I drove him to work, dropped him off. He ran in and brought me a coffee for the drive home. It was routine, but this time zero connection.

I didn't know that would be the last time I'd see him though...

Over the next week, we spoke for shorter video calls each night. We often just found each other sitting there barely speaking but just feeling the company from one another. The coming weekend was a long weekend. I was kind of hoping he would ask me to hang out. I even suggested it but he said he'd let me know. That alone screamed anxiety to me. I had family plans that weekend on two of the days, but it was a four day weekend, so there was still plenty of time. I calculated everything in my head. Four days off work. Two days with family for 3 to 4 hours each day. That's plenty of time to hang out.

I was addicted to his attention, even that week when his attention was shit.

The weekend at the first family dinner, I remember everyone noticed I seemed lighter. One described as happier even. I told my cousin across the table I had someone. Stupid, because I really didn't. I told them as much as what was appropriate. K had been texting me during dinner telling me he was going for drinks with friends in the city, not far from where I lived. I was expecting him to send me a message inviting me. That was all in my head because he never did.

I remember my cousin came around and sat next to me and asked me more questions directly about K. He knew I didn't want to really divulge every single detail about him across the entire family table. Bear in mind, my family's huge. There's probably thirty people at this long dining table, so my cousin knew it would go around the table like wildfire if we kept talking across the table.

Something that really stuck with me that he said was, "You guys keep going apart and coming back together. There's something bringing you back every time. That's strong. That's something to hold on to."

He was right. I knew it was strong. I think K knew it was strong. Why are we fighting it?

The family dinner wrapped up and I texted K to let him know

I was about to leave. No invite to drinks, I hopped in the car and drove home. I was disappointed. I thought he'd invite me. I felt a slight rejection. He was out with friends, but people I'd met, so why wasn't I allowed to come?

I got home and was angry about the whole thing, but mostly angry with myself for letting my head overthink as much as it did. I barely slept that night, but I didn't reach out to him to probe, thank god.

The following week we barely spoke. I tried, but I could also feel him completely pulling back. It was driving me insane. My anxiety was at a 10 out of 10 for the entire week. I'd never felt my anxiety take over like that. It was crazy. I barely slept any night that week. I could feel it taking over my brain like chaos. I had let the chaos take over.

I couldn't handle what was going on in my brain. It was driving me insane. I went on four 10km walks that week to try and let out the chaos from my brain but that didn't do anything. It was crippling me. What was even worse was none of my friends knew what I was going through. Or better said, what I'd put myself through. I didn't know what to do. I was ready to snap.

So, of course, I texted him. *Can we talk tonight?*

Sure.

That night, I waited for him to call or text or something. He didn't. It got to about 9p.m., I bit the bullet and called him. He was hanging out with his housemate so I knew we couldn't actually talk properly. He was deferring the conversation that we both knew had to happen, so I got off the phone after saying, "I guess we won't talk properly tonight," and hung up.

Sure, it might have been childish to hang up, but I couldn't control how I was feeling.

He texted and said, *We'll talk properly tomorrow night.*

I left it from that point on.

The next night, I waited and waited, STUPIDLY for him to call. He didn't.

The day after that, I texted saying, *So, I guess we won't talk?*

I was waiting for you to call me.

So was I.

We'd suddenly hit a huge communication flaw that I didn't think we could get ourselves back from. I could feel the rage taking over me. I was so angry I'd been completely abandoned to my own self-doubt for the last week or so. He'd left me. He'd led me on to think we were going somewhere when he knew in full reality we weren't. He always knew what I wanted from him. He knew how my brain thought. He knew of my anxiety. He knew all of this. I sat here blaming him but really I knew I was also to blame. I let the dreaming of it get the better of me. I let him back into my life. I opened back up to him. Fuck.

The next night rolled around and I texted him saying, *Let me know, when you finish work and I'll call.*

Sure, I finish at 6.

The time was 6p.m. I was waiting, then realised that was the problem for the last few days. We'd both been waiting for the other.

I sat on my couch at home, picked up the phone. Took a huge deep breath and called.

"Hey."

"Hey."

"So should I just roll straight into this?"

"Sure, let it out."

"I just want to say I want you to feel the way you want to feel with me. If you want to hold my hand, hold my hand. If you want to kiss me, kiss me. If you want to cuddle me, cuddle me. That's all I want, but instead you're scared of leading me on too quickly. What we have is what I want. Of course, eventually, I want to be dating, and I don't know if you're ready or whatever, but what I'm saying is, I've put myself out there with you and I'm giving you permission to act the way we clearly want to act with each other. All I want during this is respect. I don't want to be overthinking and I don't want you overthinking. I just want us to be us."

"Morgan, I totally get what you're saying but what you're asking me to do is literally take advantage of you. Sure, I want to have sex with you. I want to have lots of sex with you. And I want to act the way we act with each other with you. But I also want to be free and have sex with others, which if I'm doing all those things with you, isn't an option. I'm just not ready for a relationship. I'm still in the mindset that I want to be free but if and when I'm ready for a relationship, I'm telling you there's no one else I'd want to even consider it with. You're perfect, but I'm telling you I'm just not ready."

"What even is ready by this stage? It's been years of this shit K. If it's not now, it's not ever."

"I don't think that's fair. I'm going to know when I'm ready, you can't put that on me because all I know right now is that I know I'm NOT ready."

"I don't get it. This is fucked. You act the way you act with me but you don't want it properly but you still want it every single day. You've told me that. You've acted on that. But I'm obviously not enough."

"You are enough! You're more than enough! If we went out and ended up making out and sleeping together I'm saying I would totally go for it if it was mutual."

"Oh, so you're saying you'd take advantage of me when I was drunk."

"No! That's not it! I'm just saying if it was to happen like fate."

"FATE?"

"Yes!"

"So, what is it that you want?"

"Well, I'd still like to do what we're doing, but I'd like the freedom and whilst I'm free you can be too."

"What do you even mean?"

"Well, maybe we need to be more in communication about who and when we're sleeping with someone else?"

"You want me to tell you when I sleep with someone else?"

"Yeah, I don't see that being a problem! And I'll do the same for you. That way we each know everything and nothing is being hidden."

"You want me to literally report back on who I'm fucking… so you feel like you've been informed?"

"Yeah?"

"You do realise that's like an open relationship."

"Well, in a sense."

"No… you're telling me you don't want to be in a relationship with me but you want me to report back on everyone I sleep with whilst we talk so we can both be informed of the others actions, yet we're not in a relationship at all, so we can't even call it an open relationship. We're just telling the other we fucked someone else…"

"Shit."

We went around in circles. I was being pushed further and further into a dark hole that made me feel like I was worthless. I wasn't really wanted. I felt useless. I wasn't good enough. I got off the phone and immediately sat in absolute exhaustion. I was numb.

I barely slept that night.

I didn't know if there was anything else to say. He'd ended the conversation asking if we could continue to be friends and told me to take a few days to think about if it was even possible. I couldn't bear the idea of being just his friend. He knew I fucking hated whenever he'd call me that because we weren't. We were more than that!

I hated the fact that my family now knew about him. Like I had more people to explain this stupid fucking situation to. I hadn't even told a friend by this stage. Not one. I felt so embarrassed by the whole thing. Embarrassed for myself, for my family who were all excited for me. Embarrassed. Shamed.

Over the next few days, I wrote a fucking ESSAY into the notes sections on my phone. Every few hours editing it. Writing more. Removing some. Everytime, I thought it was getting better and better and more to the point. I'd never felt the need to draft anything in notes ever in my life. The only thing in my notes on my phone were grocery lists. This felt inorganic, like it wasn't me. And it wasn't. He'd led me to this point where I wasn't even being myself any more. Who the fuck was I? Who was this chaotic person?

After days and days of pondering, this was what I ended up coming up with,

K, I can't be friends with someone I love. We can't do it and we've tried and I shouldn't be asked to bottle my feelings away, until potentially a later date and literally pretend we're just friends, nor do I believe you should bottle your feelings too. You have serious commitment issues that you need to address. I understand you don't want a relationship but you don't seem to realise you've been in one. The fact you can't even let something be organic, when with us it's literally unstoppable and when you're switched on it's so amazing but when you're switched off it's fucked up, shows how you really need to finally address these issues. It's been almost three years we've known each other and this keeps happening... and I'm ready for whatever it may be, again something you can't plan or forecast, but you can't ever come back my way and switch off again and not be ready. It's been too many times but I guess you're lucky, I still believe in it. I understand, you're not ready right now, but all I can say is figure it out. You said, 'Maybe in three months, six months, five years,' to me like it was something you could plan. Being ready for something more with someone isn't a switch that'll switch itself, you have to do the work and if you need to get help, get help. I was serious when I said you have to figure out what you really want and now more than ever before because I'm saying you can't have me in your life the way you want me. Your actions and feelings with me versus your brain saying no just don't match up at all. Sure, check in once in a while and call when you really need to but you and I would be far too jealous of each other to pretend we're fine with the other knowingly sleeping or seeing or dating someone else. I know for myself, I don't even want to hear any of it. I really didn't want to lose you but I will not be asked to co-exist with you and hide how I really feel whilst you want to be a fuck boy. Figure it out before you lose me for good, which sadly, you're lying to yourself saying you're OK with.

I felt confident in that message. Sure it was long, an essay, but who cares. You've fucking driven me to this point. So read it and realise the fucking torture you've put me through time and time again. I crossed all the bases. His commitment issues. His idea of being 'ready'. The threat of me being gone for good. But most importantly, in the first few words, I'd finally admitted how I really felt. I hate to say it, but I loved him. I was in love with him. I hated him, but I loved him. That was the part about the message I was most vulnerable about. I knew the message would be a lot to digest, but I knew I needed to send it.

I hit send finally after probably five or six days of beating myself up in my brain.

My heart sank. I felt completely dead inside. My anxiety was the only thing I could feel as I sent him the message and wanted to die.

Within minutes, he'd opened it. Obviously, a lot to read, I knew it'd take a hot minute for a response.

My phone went ding. I didn't want to look at it but I had to.

OK, thank you for your honest message.

That's it. That's all I'm worth. Wow.

I didn't cry. I couldn't cry about it any more. Three years of knowing this douchebag and all I actually wanted in that moment was to burst into tears but he couldn't even give me that. I was once again numb.

I had no energy left, nothing left to overthink. I'd already over thought every single word in that fucking essay. I literally had nothing left to give the situation. Or situationship.

All I felt was chaos through my bloodstream. Anger, rage, sadness, depression, all kicking in and taking over my body. But even with all these dark emotions going through my bloodstream and taking over my body, I was just numb. Completely and utterly numb.

Over the next few days, every time my phone went off I thought it'd be him. It never was.

About two weeks later, he sent me a meme. Were we playing this game now? Just exchanging memes? Yep, I guess we were.

He'd send one.

I'd send one.

It was just playing tag but neither of us were actually saying any words to each other.

About a month later, I got a message from him.

I was just on your street.

At the time, I wasn't even home, I actually found it a little bit creepy but also like... why the fuck are you even telling me this in the first place?

I think I responded a couple of hours later or the next morning, not sure, but every scenario as to why had gone through my head. Was he sleeping with someone on my street? Was he trying to ask to come over? Every scenario.

Why?

I was with my housemate, and he was driving and he took a wrong turn.

OK.

That was it. What the actual fuck. Like why bother even telling me? Did you want me to put the kettle on and make you both a cup of tea? Get fucked.

After that, we didn't really ever speak again properly. I tried. He tried. Neither of us knew how to. I think it's impossible to speak to someone so casually when you literally never knew how to and have those feelings for each other. When you know you both want to say more but can't, it's just impossible to see eye to eye.

Morgan

Over the course of the next few months, I tried to focus on myself and what I really wanted from any potential source of love.

I found it really difficult to think about because at that time I was so deep and dark about the whole subject. I didn't know exactly what I wanted any more, all I knew was that I was somehow still open to what it could bring me.

I wasn't someone who necessarily dreamt of marriage, kids, or the white picket fence life. All I knew is I wanted to experience it with someone who I felt it for. And that's still how I feel about it. I'm open to whatever it can bring me. I just wanted to feel it, but I also knew I didn't just want any boyfriend. I wanted a partner to actually experience whatever life had to offer. The highs, the lows, whatever the fuck it was. If I wanted a boyfriend, I knew I could just find someone and have one. I never really wanted that. I wanted a partner. My partner. The right person. I was never going to just settle for a boyfriend. Never. That may be a little intense to some especially seeing as my mantra was always 'just go with it' but I think deep down it's something I always knew.

I have amazing people to look up to. My parents, married for thirty-five years, together forty. My sister and her husband. My brother and his fiancé. Why was I the one struggling so much to find that someone?

I tried looking at all the men and what they have in common. Physically, fucking nothing besides brown eyes. That seems to be the only physical feature they had in common. All of them are different.

I thought more about what traits mentally they had in common. Emotionally unavailable. One hundred per cent. That was it. I cracked the code.

Now... how the fuck do I find someone EMOTIONALLY AVAILABLE? Do I add it to my dating profiles? "Must be emotionally available." That's not gonna stop the unavailable ones at all.

There's no way to know. One minute you are available; the next, you aren't. It's like the blind leading the blind, except when you're blind, aren't you meant to have a better sense of smell? Cos I can't fucking smell it and I've been wearing glasses, since I was thirteen!

I'd sit there, back on the dreaded apps, swiping away realising I wasn't really swiping right on anyone. I had absolutely no urge for anything or anyone. I was still numb. I was getting better as time went on, especially with zero contact with K. It seemed to help.

The time was maybe late July/early August by this point. I

was thinking, *OK it's been a few months, maybe it's time to at least TRY.*

I matched with someone new. Someone who's not really my taste. I was kind of attracted to him, but not crazily. But he sparked the conversation and it seemed to flow kind of smoothly.

We spoke for a couple of days and he asked me to dinner.

Fuck it.

Yeah!

I was excited. I hadn't been asked on an actual date in a long time. K never asked me on a date. It was just casual dinners.

We met up. It was this seafood restaurant. Kinda nice, kinda casual, my style.

We had wine, we had seafood, and the conversation flowed super easy. It was organic. Something I hadn't had in a while.

We spoke about everything. Past relationships (don't worry, I only scraped the surface on that one), what we wanted from a relationship (he was a lot more specific than I was), what we were open to. The list went on.

When we left the restaurant, we walked, a bit drunk, and found a pub nearby. We sat there and kept talking for hours. It was actually really nice to be sitting across from someone talking our asses off and actually getting along.

He leant in to kiss me. I kissed him. Nice, tender, soft, easy, nothing pashy, just a cheeky kiss.

He then went to go to the bathroom, leaving my anxiety to kick in when drunk and go, *you just had your first kiss with someone new and didn't puke, go you, but was it good? Will there be another one? Did you actually like it or were you just on a high from kissing someone?*

He came back from the bathroom, both smiley, talking again nonstop.

The date was a success. I think... for now.

I was walking home that night and was kind of really happy. Something I hadn't felt in a looooong time. Something that almost felt abnormal.

I was getting close to my street all smitten and happy from the date, but then the anxiety kicked in.

I realised I was drunk. I realised it felt abnormal. But I also realised I really wasn't ready for all these feelings again.

During the dinner and drinks, two different venues and during all of the conversations and even during the kiss, I realised, it wasn't K. I was sitting across from someone who was actually amazing and presented themselves well and was ticking almost every mental box I'd had on my little mental list, but the problem was that it simply wasn't K.

I fucking hated myself. I woke up the next morning, wanting to kick myself in the head when this lovely sweet guy texted me saying,

I had a really amazing time with you.

I didn't know how to respond at all. I DID have an amazing time. I DID want to see him again. But what I DID realise is that I was still hung up on the last person who made me feel smitten and what I wanted was that date to be with that person, not this one!

I fucking hate what this date had done to me. I didn't know how to process it at all. He was actually the nicest person. We got along really well. But despite the date being actually amazing, it mentally sent me back twenty five steps. My love for K had come back to the surface. I couldn't pretend I was as happy on that date as I really was. I wasn't happy. It was with the wrong person. I wasn't fucking ready.

We did speak a bit after that, I explained I had an amazing time but I needed to take things slow because I wasn't that far out of a really confusing situationship. He completely understood and actually sympathised with me as he said he'd gone through this shit before.

CARING – TICK
UNDERSTANDING – TICK
Fuck. I couldn't do this.

We kept in contact but I didn't see him again. He asked for a second date. I blamed work and pretended I had a lot on my plate. I definitely had a lot on my plate, it wasn't all work. It was fucking anxiety and the chaos that was my dating history. I think he got the hint that I just wasn't OK to be dating.

Over the coming weeks, I spoke to my friends and family and really just focused on work and going day by day through the pain. I took the time over the next month to really focus on just going day by day through all of it. Feel the emotions. If I want to be sad, be sad. If I want to distract myself, distract myself. But I really just wanted to process what I needed to process as I've always tried to just distract distract distract and suppress suppress suppress. It was never healthy and if anything, added to the chaotic level of anxiety I'd grown to live with. I'd reached a level of anxiety that sits just before a full anxiety attack. My friends would call it 'chaos mode'. This is a level I realised I had been often sitting just under for years and with the flick of a switch I'd go full chaos mode and seek destruction. At this point I feel like it's finally simmering down.

I remember a phone call I had with my mum a few days later by the time the weekend had come.

I was aimlessly driving around the area trying to distract my brain from letting the chaos take over and she happened to call exactly when I was trying not to think about exactly what I knew she wanted to talk about.

She knew the mental pain I was going through with all my dating history. She knew it was a lot. She didn't know every detail. Actually, she barely knew any details, but it was just one of those things Mum's KNOW. They know when their babies are going through something. They can feel it. She described me as the 'dark horse' of the family, which, being the dark sided Scorpio that I am, I kind of fucking loved that idea! But it was something she felt in her core. She knew her baby wasn't doing well.

"How are you going with everything?"

"I'm OK."

"Yeah?"

"Actually, I'm really fucking over it."

"Yeah, that's what I usually think when you say you're OK."

"I'm sick of thinking I've moved on then realising I haven't."

"Well, Morgy, it's a day by day thing."

"Yeah I get that, that's what I've been working on for a while now."

"You just need to take it easy. Don't put the pressure on yourself. Your man is out there don't worry."

"But Mum, what if he's not?"

Mum's tone changed.

"What?"

"Well, what if he's not?"

"Morgy, don't say that."

"No, I mean I'll always be hopeful that he is out there, but if I'm honest, I've been trying to date for the last month, I even met a really amazing guy who I got along with really really well, but I realised later on in the night that it wasn't K."

"Morgy, this is what I mean by day by day."

"No I get it, but when is the search over? When do I know that I've met someone and won't think they're not K?"

"Well, you'll just know when you know."

"Yeah."

"No one can give you a deadline or anything for this. No one can say *this is him*. You'll just feel it when you feel it."

My mother was really amazing at listening but one thing about her is she's even better at giving me that Hallmark movie one liner that on reflection, really doesn't mean anything at all

"The sun will shine tomorrow, Morgy."

"Thanks, Mum."

"But seriously, you're an amazing person. I've learnt so much about you over the last few years. You're a deep special boy who all of these men who've treated you like shit and quite frankly, used you, all of them know that and you're too daunting to them because they see how special you are."

"… Mum that might be one of the nicest and realest things you've ever said to me."

"But it's true, you're my baby boy and I hate knowing these men have treated you like shit. They're not worth your time."

"I know that, but it's not something you can just identify quickly when you meet someone."

"No, but I know you'll find someone. I know you don't want to settle for just anyone. I know that person is out there for you."

"Thanks, Mum."

What Mum couldn't see as I was driving were the tears rolling down by face. She was right. I had someone in my corner reminding me that I was fucking amazing. Why had I lost that feeling about myself? I was open to all of the possibilities in the world with someone, but what I'd forgotten about myself is that I was still open to all the possibilities in the world even if I was by myself. It's not that I was dependant on a man making me feel whole, but it's that I'd forgotten I know how to do it on my own, that I am the fucking shit. Why had I forgotten how strong a person I was. I was technically doing it all alone the entire time.

It's funny because it's something I know about myself. It's something my friends would go, "Fuck him, you're amazing" and I knew it. But when it comes from your own mother saying it, it hits differently. It's like she knew I needed to hear it at that moment.

The phone conversation continued though.

"If I am honest though, Mum."

"Sure, go on."

"I just don't think I can keep putting myself out there the way I have been because everytime I try, I realise I'm not where I should be when trying to date."

"What are you saying, Morgy?"

"I just think I'm giving up. I don't want to try any longer. I'm just so over it."

"Well, just take it day by day and see how you feel."

"No, Mum, I think I'm just done trying altogether."

"What?"

"I know it might sound really negative, and I know I'm a catch and all, but I just frankly cannot fathom the idea of trying anytime soon, and if I had to put a timeline on it I don't think I have it in me to try again at all. It's not that I'm giving up... well actually... fuck it, yeah I'm giving up. It mightn't be forever, but I can't see it happening again anytime soon at all."

"Morgy, I don't like this."

"No, Mum, as I'm saying it I'm smiling. I feel like I actually am fine with just not trying any more. I don't want to date or try or anything. I just want to be me again and happy and if someone comes along, GREAT, but in this fucked up dating world that we live in... they won't just come along organically any more."

"What do you mean?"

"Well, the days of walking up to someone in a bar and asking to buy them a drink are over. That's considered creepy now. You have to be on the apps or whatever, open to it but all the organic ways of meeting someone are literally dead."

"So, you're just going to exist?"

"Yeah, that's it! I'm just going to exist and slowly feel like myself again. I need to remember who the fuck I am!"

Mum and I got off the phone not long after that. She went on to say she understood but was really upset and worried because she heard me closing off from the potential of being happy with someone.

She always said she saw me with a partner and being the

happiest ever and she was distraught at the idea that I was closed off from that being a possibility. Her dream of me being happy with someone over that phone call had become impossible. And if I'm honest, I kind of felt like that too.

I didn't want to be burdened by any man ever again, but I knew I wouldn't always have this mentality. I knew one day, it could be years, but one day I would be open to it again.

I didn't want to think about men for ages. I didn't want to try.

I was so sick of putting myself out there.

The next week, every morning felt a little bit easier than the one before.

I was happy again at work. People at the office noticed and everyone was asking if I'd met someone.

I hadn't! They were all surprised but when I explained I was shut off from the world of men they all went, "Fuck yeah, go you."

That week felt dark, but still lighter than it'd been for the last few months.

Day by day. I felt like I'd finally stopped thinking about men altogether, well not stopped, but stopped worrying about men. Stopped letting the chaos get to me.

I still had the apps on my phone but frankly, wasn't opening a single one of them.

I didn't want to. I'd get a notification saying, *Where've you been? There's lots of people waiting to match with you,* from one of the dating apps' automatic marketing schemes to try and get you back into their services but I'd just clear my notifications and smile and lock my phone again.

I guess it's important to actually take the time between dating people to actually observe and figure out what went wrong or what the lessons were to be learnt. Between everyone I'd ever seen or dated or whatever the fuck, I'd usually just harped on what happened but never actually processed it or grew from it. Or maybe, I never realised I was processing and learning from them. But I knew I never really took the time to feel what I needed to fully feel post break-up. Some, no growth needed, some, definitely. But I also had a mentality towards break ups or whatever I have the right to call them seeing as I've never had a real relationship… but I have the mentality that I just deal with the emotions by sweeping them under the rug and continuing to live my life until I can't remember them any more.

I would never mentally take the time to process it properly.

I'm not saying I'm the victim in all of these scenarios. There's definitely times where I've been the villain and could have acted in a different way, but that's it. It would have been an act and that's not something I can do.

I feel what I feel and I let out what is necessary.

I try to live my life as authentically as I can.

I don't want to go through life faking anything. I've known myself and been confident in who I am as a person from a younger age. I haven't always been able to confidently show it all but in recent years, I've been able to, and pretty strongly. I just need to get back to being THAT person.

Would I ever get to the point to be open to love again? I wasn't sure at that stage. Was I happy with where I sat at that exact moment in time, yes I was. I was happy on my own. I knew how to be independent. Fuck, I've been doing it all on my own my whole adult life. Deep down I also knew I would get to a point where I'd be open to love again as well, but in the process of trying to find myself again and being used to burying emotions, that was the one thing I was going to bury.

In not a single one of the stories of these men was I ever in an actual branded relationship. Not one of them was my boyfriend. None. Not a single one. Some of them I still feel the need to refer to as an ex because frankly given the time and connection, they'd broken me down enough to grant me the right to call them that.

I may not have had the right to call them a boyfriend, but I fucking earnt the right to call them an ex. That's for fucking sure.

That's the dating world we live in now. We go from one situationship to the next, and we're all fine to fall into one with the hopes of it blooming into a relationship, but from my perspective at least, it never does, or hasn't yet.

Do I need to re-enter the dating world in the future with a t-shirt that says 'Open to a relationship, you must be too'.

Was it that easy and direct?

No way, that's embarrassing. But what was the trick?

I was sick of wondering. Sick of trying to crack the code. I was even more sick of people saying, "When you meet them, you'll just know."

KNOW WHAT?

I was at a point, where I was severely over it and over wondering when he'll turn up. Who was this mysterious person who would just show up in my life one day and everything would change? Who was this magical creature? I knew I had to shift my idea of waiting for him to him waiting for me. I had to start thinking that I was the mysterious person who would just show up in someone's life one day and change it. I was the magical creature. I was the prize at the end of the day. That was it. Shift the mental focus. Enough of beating myself down to think they're the one to wait for. What if I'm the one they should be fucking waiting for. I'm the catch at the end of the day. I'm the prize. I'm the one that's worth it.

I still wanted my romance. I wanted my damn romantic comedy starring Drew Barrymore and Adam Sandler except I WANTED TO BE DREW BARRYMORE.

I wanted my perfect version of Dan Levy, my celebrity crush, telling me that I'm beautiful and everything he'd been looking for in life. I wanted my fucking romance.

And from what I'd been told a million times by my friends and family, apparently I deserved it. I just needed to get to a point where I really believed I deserved it as well.

The next week, I could feel myself actually getting hopeful again. It was like it'd just popped into my bloodstream again and I was smiling and feeling myself a little bit more.

Was I open to a relationship, I mean, always, but was I open to looking for it? Nope! But the fact I could feel within myself that this romantic side of me was still there and present, that felt amazing. The hope was brewing within me again and that's the progress I needed.

I don't want to end this saying that I'm dead inside and never going to be open to looking for him again. I want to believe he's out there for me. Through all of this, I truly do believe in love, I really do. I just don't believe the love I'm seeking and am after has come my way yet. But I still believed it would. I'm just fucking impatient. Something I've known about myself from a REALLY young age. I really am impatient as fuck.

I believe in it probably more than anything in life. My career, sure, it's great. My friends, amazing, love them all. Everything will always be stable and good. But my belief for finding this true love that I've always dreamt of, sure it dwindles every now and then away from me, but overall I still believe in it and the one thing through all of this is that I know I will always have hope.

I hope it comes. I hope it presents itself in my little chaotic life. I have a good enough perspective to know I'm no one in this world. I'm just like another little ant living on the planet trying to make do with what I can create of it. But I'm hopeful, I can be tiny on this planet with someone's hand in my hand at some point.

But it's my chaotic life. It's my chaos. And I want someone to embrace it with me, not fear it. Whether your chaos is your family with three kids, your chaotic career, or like myself, your love life, it's there. We all have chaos, but I'm now trying to own it for what it is.

I applied this outlook onto my life for the next while. Embracing my chaos. Whatever it be. I loved it, I felt like I was actually on top of it all, enjoying my time again.

Really, I'm not lying!

September came and I was enjoying my time, enjoying my friends, laughing and having fun. I wasn't trying with guys, but I could feel the hope within me really coming back.

I want to end this knowing I'm not leaving anything on a downward spiral.

I haven't got anything I thought I'd have by the time, I'm finishing this at thirty years old. Yes. Thirty. A gay man at thirty,

I may as well just die now shouldn't I? Well, the one thing I do have that I definitely didn't think I'd have is a little bit of trauma. The other thing I know I've got is my hope. No one will ever fucking take that from me.

You can beat me down, mentally make me spiral like I'm the crazy one, but what I'll always have is my hope and I'll hold that with me through every aspect of my life.

Sorry, back to the part where I was enjoying my time with my friends and laughing *yada yada* you know. I was happy. I just know I could be happier. I was independent, I was good. I'm doing fine and that's OK!

I was living my life, enjoying it for what it was finally. Something I hadn't had the mental capacity to do in a long time. I was on a high, knowing I still had my hope despite feeling like every one of these guys were stripping it from me bit by bit.

Nothing and no one could take that away and frankly I wouldn't let them. Fuck anyone that would ever try to take that away from me. Some of the men in these stories included.

To all the single people out there who feel like they've lost their hope, just know that you haven't. It dwindles and goes away from time to time, but it will never ever be completely gone. It just won't. It'll be buried deep inside of you and feel like it's gone, but it's not. You have to have hope for whatever it is used for. Everytime, you watch a romantic movie and end up crying… or if you're like me, bitterly yelling, "OH FUCK OFF," at the TV screen, that's literally your hope coming out. It may not always show in a happy format, that's normal, but the tears or the yelling are reactions based on it coming out. If you have a thought or feeling like that, it's literally your hope saying, "I'm still here." Know that. Remember that. And even more importantly, feel it.

Ignore all the hallmark bullshit advice that people say to make you feel hopeful when we all know it doesn't do shit. Just know you don't need those inspirational quotes in order to still feel the hope that's within yourself. Scream at the fucking TV! Cry! Literally, just fucking feel it!

Just know that me saying all of this shit doesn't take away from the fact I'm still in the same fucking boat that I was in at the beginning, just with a lot more crazy bullshit stories to tell.

Hey, at least most of these stories I can laugh about now!

But what's most important to remember from all of this is you can be torn down,
left broken-hearted,
thrown to the side for a while,
made to feel like absolute shit,
made to feel unwanted,
told *NO* a hundred times,
or that they're not ready,
or that they don't know what they want,
OR that you've shown them what they want they just don't know if they want it,
OR it's not the right time,
OR you're exactly the boyfriend they want they just don't deserve it,

OR whatever fucking bullshit excuse you've heard before just repeated from a different entity.

Woh! Back to the point Morgan, sorry everyone, but what's most important to know... you need to have hope.

If I can still have it, even if it's just one per cent, that's my fucking one per cent. Not theirs, not yours, it's mine. I'm keeping it. I'll charge it when I can. But it's not a phone. It won't die and stay turned off. It'll actually stay at the one per cent it's meant to stay at. And if it's at one per cent, let it stay there for a bit. Don't rush to plug it straight in and quickly charge it up to hundred per cent. Just let it be one per cent, if you need it to be. The hope won't die.

I may have been told all of those above disappointing lines a hundred times but my hope still runs through my body. Through my veins. Right now it's not that strong, but I can still feel it. I know it's there. Call me a hopeless romantic. I don't care. But to be honest, I'd rather be called a hopeful romantic.

I have hope that he's out there for me. I have hope that he exists. I have hope that whatever presents itself in the future will actually look at me like the fucking GOD that I am and actually appreciate and treat me like I should be. And I will treat them the same way. It's out there. It's got to be out there. I can't feel all this love within myself for no reason. I'm meant to give it to someone. I'm meant to share it. I want to share it.

Life was going well at this point. My hope was charging again. Was I out in the world seeking it? No, I wasn't. Was I thinking of myself as the prize finally? Yes, I was. I was finally treating myself with the respect that I should have been treating myself with the entire time! Was I finally getting it? I think I was. I believed I was. I was finally feeling like myself again.

Everyone around me could feel it coming through me. Radiating through my pores and skin. I was finally being Morgan again. Being myself. Happy, laughing, smiling non-stop. It took a while, but I needed it to take a while to get myself back.

And then in September… when I was finally feeling like myself again…

I met <u>him</u>.